# BENCH MARKS

# BENCH
# MARKS

*15727*

*by József Farkas*

TRANSLATED BY JOHN R. BODO

**JOHN KNOX PRESS**
Richmond, Virginia

Standard Book Number: 8042-2020-4
Library of Congress Catalog Card Number: 69-12847
© M. E. Bratcher 1969
Printed in the United States of America

# CONTENTS

•

# STAGES ALONG THE WAY

Matthew 5:17–20

If my task were a theological lecture on these four verses, I should be able to set forth a good deal of interesting information. I would have to discuss the problems of the relationship between Jesus of Nazareth and the Old Testament law, the Torah, and what Jesus thought of Moses and of the observance of the Hebrew law.

And I would have to say something about the earliest Christian congregations that set themselves apart more and more from the Jews. What was the relationship between them and the law of Moses?

I would have to identify the party with whom our Scripture lesson is quarreling. "Think not that I have come to abolish the law and the prophets . . ." (R.S.V.). Apparently there were some who held this opinion. Who were these people?

Furthermore: "Whoever then relaxes one of the least of these commandments and teaches men so . . ." (R.S.V.). Who were these false teachers who encouraged such a relaxed version of the law?

These would be but a few of the exciting professional problems with which I would have to deal. But such is not my task. That is the task of biblical scholarship.

My present task is to proclaim the Word of God, to set forth God's message for us in relation to this particular passage. Therefore, I will not go into any detail with respect to scholarly questions.

Instead I will pose a problem of universal scope, and while seeking an answer to this problem I will have occasion to deal with our text. Then I will try to blend the message of the text into the answer to the universal problem.

The universal problem is this: *How does man become human?*

This is a question we indeed must raise. It is not enough for us to ask how a man becomes a Christian. This narrower question is closer to our hearts; it is familiar to us. But let us remember that God has designed our mission for a larger territory!

How does man become human? Scholars generally contend that the process of humanization has been completed. Some time, many thousands of years ago, man became human, and human history has been unfolding ever since.

Everyone tends to answer the question according to his own world view. Man became man by coming down from the tree, by making tools, by starting to work. Or man became human when he began to talk; speech started the life of the spirit. Or, again, man became human when he began to pray, when he first sought to make contact with the superhuman, the transcendent. There are other answers, of course, but the consensus is that the process of humanization ran its course long ago and that now we are human.

In a sense this is true. But let me confess to you my conviction that the process of becoming human is still going on. Thousands of years ago something happened for the sake of our becoming human. To be sure, we have not taken many steps in that direction. Thousands of years of human life are behind us, and it is our hope that other thousands of years are ahead of us. We have a long way to go before man becomes truly human.

Let me offer just one illustration. Everyone recalls with horror the cannibals who would club a man to death and then eat him. We feel that this is behavior unworthy of human beings, subhuman behavior which, thank God, we have left behind. Today we are truly men. But I am troubled by the question whether the difference is really so convincing. The cannibal killed and ate one or two or ten others. But today, thanks to technology, it is possible to kill millions all at once, always with a suitable ideological justification: they are our enemies; they are endangering our lives. The action

is buttressed by appropriate reasons. It is allegedly a "fact" that
they must be killed. And technology has made the killing possible
—the destruction of millions at the push of one or two buttons.
Have we really risen above cannibalism? I do not think so. Neither
our rationalization of the massacre of millions nor the ease with
which the massacre can be carried out is any proof of our further
humanization! Becoming human is a long hard process, the history
of millenia. And we must admit that we are stumbling about at the
very beginning of this process.

However, this problem must not be viewed only in its cosmic
dimensions, in terms of the life of mankind. It is certain that all
mankind is involved, but I am convinced that every one of us
individually has to go through this process. This is a school in which
each one of us must enroll, and in which we must, as individuals,
earn some degree in becoming human. The fact that we are not
illiterates—that we can read and write—that we may even have a
high school or university diploma—does not in any way guarantee
that we have become human.

Becoming human is something entirely different.

I would like to give an account now of what, according to my
belief, experience, and observation, constitutes becoming human.
Specifically, I would like to indicate three stages in the process. In
this way, we will also be dealing with the text for the day.

The first stage is this: Man becomes aware of law, order, truth,
and strives to fit into the law. Thus begins the process by which
he becomes human. Man realizes that there is a universal order
which governs not only the course of the stars but also the life of
man, man's common life, and that it is not possible to sin with
impunity against this invisible, immovable order. When man seeks
this eternal order, when he tries to come to terms with it, he has
made a beginning in the process of humanization. This applies to
all mankind and it applies to each of us individually. Through the
ages, man has been seeking, deciphering, groping for, this order,
which is the everlasting law of life, of man's common life.

In this quest, the figure of Moses stands out. Not he alone, to
be sure, but he is remarkable as a seeker of this order, because he

received a revelation. The law, the Torah, is indeed the framework of the divine order; and it was God's great gift to the Jewish people that they were permitted to recognize this order.

Unfortunately, however, this divine order got into human hands. It got into the hands of priests, scribes, Pharisees, who began to tinker with it. They began to explain it, to whittle it, to rearrange it. They took it so well in hand that they rendered it nearly unrecognizable. The Jews are rightly proud to have received the divine law, but they have been rightly criticized for the way in which they have dealt with it. They twisted it for the benefit of their priests. They made it relative. Then came Jesus—and now we are getting at our text—and he said, "Think not that I have come to abolish the law . . ."

Jesus says yes to the Torah, but dialectically. He often says yes to the Torah while saying no to *explanations* of the Torah. In the Sermon on the Mount we can observe this dialectic point by point: "You have heard that it was said to the men of old, 'You shall not kill . . .' But I say to you that every one who is angry" has killed. "You have heard that it was said, 'You shall not commit adultery.' But I say to you that every one who looks at a woman lustfully has already committed adultery with her in his heart" (R.S.V.).

In other words, Jesus says yes to the Torah, to God's order. But in order to bring to life the original meaning of the Torah, he often took issue with the Pharisees and their explanations. This they could not forgive him; and in the end they condemned him to death as one who had transgressed the law.

Man, then, becomes human by seeking God's order and striving to fit into it. Jesus Christ is the supreme guide in our quest for God's order. He helps us to recognize God's order and his help often takes the form of exposing misconceptions.

One such misconception is that God's law can be cut down to size, our size. The Pharisees were forever whittling away at the law, and this Jesus set himself sharply against. He said, for example, "You fuss about cases of divorce. But I say to you that in the mind of God there is no room at all for divorce. God in his mercy may grant a concession to your hard hearts, but his order is constancy, fidelity. In the mind of God there is no divorce." Thus Jesus exposes all our attempts at bargaining, at cutting down God's law to our size, at adapting it to our convenience.

The phrase "I am doing all right!" expresses another of the misconceptions Jesus exposed: "I am doing my best, I'm taking the law seriously, I'm being successful at obeying God's commandments. I am interpreting them strictly and I'm keeping them!"

Here again Jesus had a sharp battle with the Pharisees. They were traveling on a road which we dare not use if he is near.

These then are two things Jesus does: He sharpens the law by insisting that this and nothing less is the will of God; and he puts an end to all Pharisaic games of hide-and-seek—that we're doing all right, we're keeping the law. He exposes the religious pride and self-righteousness that lurk in our hearts. He makes it clear that we are utterly unable to keep the law.

On the basis of certain personal experiences I now contend that the process of becoming human must include an experience of *despair*—"I want to, but I can't!" Anyone who does not reach this point, who comes by his religion and morality more cheaply, is on the wrong road—is not truly on the way to becoming human. To put it differently: Jesus simplified the law so that all that remained was the commandment to love. *Only* to love; that is all.

The matter can be discussed in a number of ways, but its essence is that we must love God and one another. That is the entire law! But . . . are you not aware of the fact that we are unable to do even that? We are not able to do even this little thing—which is not so little really, because it is everything! Anyone who realizes that God's whole will is for us to love has made a beginning in the process of becoming human. But even this we are unable to do.

The second stage is this: The same Jesus who has brought God's order *comforts* us in this despair. Are you familiar with this experience? For this is the second stage in the process of becoming human. I seek God's order, I try to fit into it, I fail, I despair. But then I receive the comfort of Jesus. The forgiveness of sins, to use the theological term. Jesus releases us: "Your sins are forgiven." This does not mean that we have a right to be flippant. Woe to him who misinterprets forgiveness as an occasion for license, as an encouragement to sin. The forgiveness of sins is essentially consolation. Jesus consoles the despairing man who wants to keep the law but cannot; the man who really wants to love everyone, including his enemies—not whittle down God's will so that he may love only two or three persons whom he finds attractive. He wants to love but he cannot. So he despairs. Eventually he says, "I am unable to live a human life; I don't have what it takes." Anyone who despairs of himself in this way will be comforted by Jesus.

Such are the strange turns and twists of our lives that at first the Word of God, the law of God, accuses us as if God himself were accusing us, and we are busy defending, explaining, ourselves. "O God," we say, "you are strict. It is impossible that you should demand so much. Furthermore I am really doing quite a lot . . ." Let us observe the life of our spirits. At first God accuses and we defend ourselves. Then as we progress, the roles are reversed. We begin to accuse ourselves. We say, "Who am I anyway? Wretched man that I am!" And at that point God begins to defend us. He says, "You are my child. Don't despair. Keep going!"

This is the second great service of Jesus Christ. His first service is to humble us in our pride, to convince us that we have nothing to brag about, that we are miserable creatures, like the animals. He humiliates us with the law. But then the same Jesus lifts us up and comforts us. He says to us, "Don't give up; keep going even if you have stumbled! It is now clear that your heart is evil; nevertheless keep willing, keep acting, keep striving, and be comforted!" This is the second stage in the process of becoming human.

And the third stage is this: that Jesus offers *hope*. He gives us hope that, even though we are not doing well today and perhaps not even tomorrow, our lives are lived in the dimension of eternity, and someday we will be doing all right. But God's message of hope is addressed only to those who are really trying and who have despaired and then received comfort from Jesus, and who are thus ready to receive the assurance that, while things are not going well now, someday they will be. There is an important biblical truth which can determine our entire life: It is not the *results* of our striving that are decisive but their *direction*, our commitment to follow Jesus. This matter of direction is decisive for all human life, though there are indeed many steps which must follow the initial step. But the number of steps is not decisive. What is decisive is whether we have set our lives in the direction of Jesus Christ.

When you think about the life eternal, don't try to figure out the extent to which you have become a saint here on earth. Just ask yourself: Have I really started on the road toward becoming human?

And now I proclaim to you this special grace: It is enough if in this life you have set your aim sincerely and decisively toward Jesus. It is enough if you have said, "Jesus, in thee alone is life; it is thee I want to follow." If you have thus set your direction, God will take hold of your hand and guide you; and you will get there.

Ponder, then, these three stages in the process of becoming human. Man becomes human by seeking God's order. In Jesus, this order is present. Man wants to fit into this order but realizes that he cannot. The requirement is simple—all he needs to do is to love. But he cannot love according to God's norm. So he despairs. But then he can receive God's comfort. He can receive forgiveness of sins as well as hope: someday he will be able.

Just decide on the direction. God will accomplish the rest!

# THE TEN COMMANDMENTS: TEN HELPS

EXODUS 20:1–17

GALATIANS 3:1–2, 24–27

During the eighteen years I have been preaching to this congregation, I have preached approximately 2500 sermons. But not one of them dealt with the Ten Commandments. I preached about fifty series of sermons, addressing a single theme for a week at a time, but the Ten Commandments never had a turn. I want to give an account of why this has been so.

It has been a basic principle with me that in a Christian pulpit we must preach Jesus, not the law. I have been obedient to this principle throughout the eighteen years. I have preached Jesus Christ, the gospel, the grace of God, not the law.

I might add to our statistics that I have preached on the glorious story of the Prodigal Son at least once every year, both singly and within various series. If it is permissible so to contrast portions of God's Word, it is my conviction that from a Christian pulpit we should much rather preach on the parable of the Prodigal Son than on the Ten Commandments. Of course, not everyone feels this way. But I am convinced that I'm thinking biblically.

Moralizing, ethical preaching, is one of the fundamental shortcomings of Christian churches. The majority of Christians—preachers included—talk about the law as if the Apostle Paul had never walked among us, as if he had never clarified the role of the law in the life of a Christian man for us. We hear the law being preached with disregard for Paul in many denominations—Roman Catholic, Baptist, Reformed—even though our inheritance from Jesus Christ is that we must preach the grace of God.

This state of things has arisen in the churches as well as in the minds of believing individuals as a result of an overly primitive theological insight that might be stated this way: It was God who gave us the Ten Commandments. This collection of rules which give direction to man's whole life is a wonderful treasure. God gave them to us that we should obey them. He who obeys them is a God-fearing man, a good Christian. He who obeys them will be saved; he who breaks them will be damned.

This is the simplified insight by which men live. No doubt it is present in your minds, too. From this insight comes such bragging as, "I am a good man; I have not stolen, I have not killed, I have not committed adultery, and so forth; therefore, God can do me no harm."

A further misconception is that of course we are human, frail men. Therefore we are not doing too well. But God is good, and no doubt he will make allowances for the little by which we fall short of complete obedience to the Ten Commandments.

This is popular theology. But I say that such theology has nothing whatever to do with Christianity. I have deliberately refrained from preaching on the Ten Commandments because I wanted to avoid the possibility that someone might misunderstand me, that he might think I was preaching this primitive theology. This is not Christianity. Christianity is not a religion of the law. It is a religion of grace. And this is how these two religions differ. The essence of a religion of law is that man wants to obey the law and thus come into God's presence. The essence of a religion of grace is that the outcome hinges not upon man's conduct but upon the love of God. The religion of law honors a strict, somber God who sits in the judgment seat like the presiding judge of a court. He keeps track of how many commandments we have observed and how many we have broken, and he pronounces sentence on this basis. He watches us passively and then proceeds to judge us.

But this is not Christianity. Christian faith presents a God who is a loving Father, who comes to our aid, who makes the first move, who smooths the path before us, who offers comfort, pardon, and strength. This, in the language of the Bible, is the grace of God—this gracious first move of God. Christianity is a religion of grace, which means that the decisive thing is not what man does—as if our salvation depended upon our actions—but what God did. For salvation is from God. And what God did was to send Jesus. Jesus took our sins upon himself. He brought us medicine and light. He came to us as a friend, a pastor. Through Jesus Christ, God grasps the hand of clumsy, lame, sinful man and heals him, comforts him, guides him. Christianity is the sum total of these gracious acts of God. When we have accepted what God has done on our behalf, *then* we may begin to respond, then we may begin to offer some token of gratitude for all that God has done for us.

I would like this Christian congregation to understand that Christianity is not a multitude of commandments which we must somehow obey, or that such obedience is really Christianity. I would have you understand that this is an error. The essence of Christianity is that God is our loving Father; he loves us; he makes the first move toward us; he helps us; and then we respond to him. But the decisive thing is that *it is God who makes the first move.*

Thus we come to the words of Paul. "O foolish Galatians! Who has bewitched you . . . ?" (R.S.V.). Something had gone wrong in the congregation in Galatia. Let us see what happened. Paul had appeared in Galatia and had begun to preach. Did he preach the Ten Commandments? Far from it! He preached Jesus Christ. So now he is saying, "Who has bewitched you, before whose eyes Jesus Christ was publicly portrayed as crucified?" (R.S.V.). This shows exactly what happened. Paul came to Galatia and preached Christ. And, in preaching the life of Jesus Christ, he concentrated on the events of the last week: the crucifixion and the resurrection. Paul proclaimed Christ. This filled the hearts of the Galatians with joy. It gave them new life. It made them brothers. It welded them into a congregation. All these things Paul sums up by saying, "You received the Holy Spirit. You received the Spirit." Paul is saying, "You foolish Galatians, whatever happened to you? Remember: I appeared in your midst, I preached Christ to you, you received the Spirit. This is the essence of Christianity. The Holy Spirit, the Spirit of God, the light, the spirit of brotherhood, of love, of peace, was poured out upon you. An outpouring of special divine power forged you into one body. You became new men. Remember, foolish Galatians, how you received the Holy Spirit. Did you receive it while trying to obey the law?"

No, Christianity appeared in Galatia when Paul preached Christ, the gospel, forgiveness of sins, the new life; and God blessed his preaching by pouring out his Spirit upon the Galatians. In a modern idiom, a new field of force appeared. The powers of light, of divine love, of God, went to work. But as soon as this happened and Paul went on his way so that he might render the same service elsewhere, some fanatical adherents of the law arrived from Jerusalem and infiltrated the congregation. They began to make trouble by saying, "What Paul has been preaching is not enough. It is both true and not true. It is true if it is followed by the circumcision, the Sabbath, the law of Moses." They said to the people, "Be careful, you can be saved only if you add the law to everything you have been hearing from Paul."

Turmoil and uncertainty followed. Word soon reached Paul that the congregation at Galatia was being shaken in its faith. This greatly saddened Paul; indeed, it made him bitter. "Is it not dreadful," he thought, "that they should thus destroy what I have built? And they believe that the law is the higher truth!"

So this is why Paul is writing, "O foolish Galatians . . . Did you receive the Spirit by works of the law, or by hearing with faith?" (R.S.V.). "Did you not receive the Holy Spirit by looking at Jesus, and by listening to preaching about him? Were not your hearts invaded by the power of God while I was revealing to you the secrets of Jesus? Do you not understand that power comes from preaching which presents Jesus Christ?"

Let us distill the essence of this ancient conflict. We can put it this way: Where the Spirit of God is poured out there is Christianity. Christianity is wherever the Holy Spirit flows into the life of men, pervading them wholly, making them new. Christianity, then, is not a series of human strivings but a series of divine blessings. It is not a process of climbing from the bottom up, but rather a reaching down of God's love by which he grasps us in the depths and lifts us out. Paul says, "You received the Holy Spirit." He asks, "How did this happen? Was it a result of your strivings, a result of your attempts to obey the Ten Commandments? Or did it happen when you were looking at Jesus and listening to testimony concerning him? Is it not then that the power of God was poured out upon you?" I will say it once more: Christianity is wherever the power of God is stirring; and the power of God will not stir just because man is striving to obey the commandments. It will stir only where Jesus Christ is being preached.

I have not preached about the Ten Commandments, because of my conviction that no matter how hard I try to hammer the Ten Commandments into your heads, no Holy Spirit and no congregation will result, since a congregation is created only by glorying in Jesus Christ.

But at this point you may ask, "If this be true, what is the significance of the law? Why are the Ten Commandments in the Bible? Surely the law must play some part in the life of the Christian!" Yes indeed. But its significance is far more modest than we give it credit in our oversimplified, vulgar theologizing. The law does indeed play a part and I would like to explain now, in an elementary way, what this part is. I am convinced that if we put the law in its place, its part in the Christian life becomes apparent. I might even pick up the Ten Commandments and preach through them, but not without first clarifying the role of the law. And I will say it again: The law is not in its place if we believe that we obtain salvation by obeying it. That is an error. When we understand that we are saved by the grace of God, then we may proceed to find out what, within this grand thought, within God's saving love, is the part of the Ten Commandments. Within this perspective, the law has a modest significance, and I would like to tell you something about the nature of this modest significance for the Christian life.

The big mistake of Christendom during the past century was to take the Ten Commandments out of their biblical context. It was said that the Hebrew context, the Hebrew environment, is not important. This mistake was made on the grandest scale in Hitler's Germany: Moses does not matter. What matters is that we have received God's eternal commandments. Let us not talk about Moses; rather, let us make these ten mighty truths the foundation of a code of law and let us live our lives according to it. In other words, the Ten Commandments were taken out of their entire historic context. It was alleged that the commandments were independent of the Jewish people, that they were everlastingly valid.

A pleasing thought, except that it does not happen to be true. The Ten Commandments make no claim to be the fundamental law for all mankind. Our fellow Christians made their mistake when they did not take the *first* sentence of the Ten Commandments seriously. Let us listen to it again: "I am the LORD your God, who brought you out of the land of Egypt, out of the house of bondage" (R.S.V.). Therefore the very text of the Ten Commandments makes it plain that it was God who first did something, and that only then did he demand a response from his people. God brought his people out of Egypt. "See what I have done for you? Now, in response to what I have done for you, enter into a covenant relationship with me and conduct yourselves thus and thus."

This is the starting point which we dare not neglect—that God delivered his people and that the Ten Commandments came in the context of the covenant. Anyone God did not deliver from Egypt should not be subject to the Ten Commandments. "Men! Jews! Remember what I have done to you! Then live your life according to this memory." This is the everlasting connection. God delivers us and then he expects us to live according to this deliverance.

Let us look at this matter in a modern perspective, because this is basic for our understanding of the law as a part of our understanding of the Bible. If you understand this, you understand all of Christianity. So let me offer a modern illustration. A few years ago I was able to save someone from dire misery. He was on the brink of suicide. God blessed my pastoral service, and I was successful in bringing him out of the depths. I did something for him. You should see the gratitude in his heart, in his eyes! Whatever I ask of him, he does at once—and he always does more than I ask of him. Another will not do half as much for me, no matter how insistently I ask. Why? Because I had given him something beforehand; I had comforted him; I had helped him. He is alive because

I was able to save him from death; and from this depth of joy he waits upon my every thought. He keeps finding new ways to demonstrate his gratitude.

This is the meaning of the law, and this is all of Christianity! God delivers us from death, and those who come through experience the birth of gratitude in their hearts so that they begin to wait upon God's will. "Lord, what can I do for thee to demonstrate my thankfulness?" This is the foundation of the Christian faith. God saves us from sin and damnation, and our joy at this deliverance motivates us to do God's will. But why should anyone do God's will whom God did not save, who did not live through this experience? This is the root of our modern nihilism which does not want to hear about God or about the Ten Commandments.

May I offer another, even more modern illustration from the life of present-day China? Friends of mine who have traveled there have told me some interesting things. One day that great idol of the Chinese, Mao, issued a decree: "Flies spread all kinds of disease; therefore, let us exterminate them." He gave the order. He laid down the law. It was apparently a startling experience when 600 million people began to kill flies. Public officials, teachers, engineers, streetcar conductors—all were killing flies, because the great Mao had ordered them to do so. Then they went on to exterminate all sparrows for the same reason.

Do you understand the connection? The people of China obeyed the law as a result of their devotion to Mao. First Mao had said, "Mothers, bear children, because we need many Chinese children." Then it developed that there were too many children. So now the word is, "Mothers, do not bear so many children, because the development of our country is being threatened!" And the mothers are not bearing children.

Again it is the connection that is important. There is someone who possesses supreme *authority*, so that when he says something, it must be done. Whether the order in itself is good or bad is not at issue. What matters is not whether the law is important or sensible or useful or difficult or easy, but that someone has ultimate authority. Thus our story furnishes a parable with respect to the place of the law. What matters is *who* says it! Obedience to the law stems from the people's devotion to the giver of the law. The

Chinese people accepted Mao's orders not because they understood their significance, but because of their devotion to him.

This is the nature of things in the Bible. God said, "Do not eat pork." That is the commandment. The Jews did not examine it as to its reasonableness or unreasonableness: "It was the same God who brought us out of Egypt, who said it; therefore we are obeying. What matters is that the same God who brought us out of Egypt commanded it." And if this state of things falls apart, nothing of value remains. This is the secret of our modern morality or immorality. God has ceased to exist; he no longer lives for modern man; but at the same time politicians and sociologists are saying, "Preserve the purity of marriage! Do not lay hands on the people's property!" They are laying down the law, but who are they? If the words are not God's words, why should we obey them? We might as well admit that we do not obey the law because we see its value. We obey it because we love the law-giver, but if we do not love him, we will not obey the law, no matter how much sense it makes.

In the Bible, then, we do not encounter an immovable order with which we must comply. Anyone who preaches along these lines does not have the faintest notion of what Christianity is. Rather, we must look to God who has brought us out of the depths, who has given Jesus Christ for us, and then, in remembrance of God's love, we begin to ask ourselves, "If God loves me so much, how does he want me to live?" And at this point, when I want to respond to God's love with gratitude, the law appears in some form.

The experience of deliverance comes first. We realize that God has brought us out of Egypt, out of despair, out of our orphan existence, our carnality, our worship of money, out of the desert of the life of average men, and has given us new life. Then the question arises, "How shall I live this new life?" And then the commandments appear to illumine our quest for this new life. They offer divine help, because they light the flame of spiritual truth in our hearts. Yes, this is the will of God, and out of love for him I want to move in this direction, live this kind of life in his presence. But the secret of salvation is not fulfillment of the law. The secret of salvation is that God loves me and gives his life to me and for me, through Jesus Christ.

In the course of my pastoral work, I often meet cases that

clearly demonstrate what misery results from an improper concept of the place of the law. Tortured lives unfold before me and, time and again, the following situation comes to light. There are parents who are serious, believing people, "biblical people," who have experienced something of God's love, have "received the Holy Spirit," and have fitted themselves into God's order. But then they try to force this order, this way of life, upon their children who have not received God's Spirit. And the result is unspeakable misery. The parents have heard the gospel and it has warmed their hearts: "Jesus gave his life for us, what might we do to serve him?" So they live lives of self-control. They tithe. But then they try to force this style of life on their children, who have not experienced the love of God, but are attracted to the world, the movies, cars. They try to press upon their children's backs the yoke of the law which they themselves are wearing with the help of the Spirit of God. The children resist for a while, then they rebel; and often the more believing the parents, the more rebellious and atheistic the children. This is what happens when we try to make people submit to the law without benefit of the Spirit.

If we contemplate this typical situation, we soon learn the ground rule of Christian nurture (if there is such a thing) that the task of parents is not to bring their children under the law but to help them receive the Spirit. Somehow parents must help their children to come under the Spirit's influence. Christian faith cannot be acquired by a rote learning of the Ten Commandments! Christian faith is to love Jesus. Think: Does humanity have any greater master than Jesus? If you know of one, follow him. I know that there is none greater. After two thousand years, his truth is timelier than ever. Beloved, I would follow Jesus Christ. I am not doing very well, but he has captivated my heart and I know that he is right! What we should try to transmit to our children is love for Jesus Christ and some of the strength which comes from Jesus Christ. He who receives this love and this strength will want to fit into the discipline which Jesus Christ expects. Salvation does not come through the law. First we receive the love of God, and obedience is born in response to this love.

Let me close with a personal confession and while I confess, think whether your experience does not match mine. For my experience is that I have tried to lead an honorable, moral, and obedient life *to the extent* that I love God, to the extent that I really feel in my heart a great desire to follow Jesus more faithfully because of the great good he has done for me. It is the love of Jesus Christ which keeps me out of mischief! Woe to me if it is the threat of damnation that keeps me from sinning! Woe to those preachers who frighten us with damnation. This is a dreadful thing! Do you think that God takes any pleasure in people who do not sin because they are afraid of damnation? I do not believe in such a God. God is pleased when someone loves him, when someone loves him even though he is stumbling. God delights more in such stumbling love than in any teeth-gnashing service.

God loves us and he strives to win our love so that we may obey him out of love rather than out of any dread of the law. The essence of Christianity is the love of God. In this love there is resolution, there is reconciliation. And the proper response to this love is, "Lord, I would like to be a worthier child of thine. I'm not worthy to be called thy son." When the desire to obey springs from a sincere love for God, God is pleased. When I am drenched through and through by the love of God, I would like to serve him all the way to a martyr's death. But if I stray from Jesus, I will soon be asking myself, "Why? When everyone is running after money and fun, why may not I?"

Look honestly into your hearts and see whether this is not the way it goes: When the image of God fades, the question appears, "Why should I be moral? Why should I be honest?" No, an honest, moral life is only possible, to whatever extent, as long as the love of Jesus Christ is vibrantly alive within us. And if we want to transmit anything to our children, let it not be the law but the love of God in Jesus Christ. Let it be the gospel, because it is out of the gospel that a life worthy of the gospel arises!

Biblical scholars have proven that originally the divine revelation engraved upon those two stone tablets was not known as Ten Commandments but simply as *Ten Words*. Keeping in mind God's original purpose rather than centuries of misuse, we may boldly call these ten words *ten helps*. And this is the crux of the matter: God is working at the redemption of his chosen people. To those whom, by divine power and his "strong right arm," he has delivered from the realm of sin, demons, slavery, hate, and violence, he offers help, in ten different ways, for their walk in the new life. He lights a flame in their hearts. He awakens a desire in them. He strengthens their will. He cultivates in them self-knowledge, penitence, humility. If we can conceive as ten *helps* what we have come to know as ten hard *laws*, then it may be worth our while to examine them more thoroughly. In this way these ten words of God may become a blessing for us. On this path let us now set our feet!

# I

## YOU SHALL HAVE A GOD!

EXODUS 20:2–3

"I am the LORD your God, who brought you out of the land of Egypt, out of the house of bondage. You shall have no other gods before me" (R.S.V.).

God's chosen people have known the Ten Commandments for three thousand years. Throughout this long time, Jews and Christians have been in entire agreement in that, when it came to explaining the Ten Commandments, they approached their task *from God's end.* This approach may be summarized as follows: God is in heaven. Men, be careful, there are not many gods, only one. This God is a strong, mighty God. Woe to him who falls into the hands of this angry God. Look out, men; be sure to get on the right side of this God. Win and hold fast to his love. This great and only God has revealed his will. Submit to his will, or you're in trouble!

In other words, the traditional approach to the Ten Commandments has been from God's end. "Men, beware! Obey! Otherwise, you will find yourself face-to-face with an angry God!"

Thousands of years passed, and, for a while, the approach worked. But I say that today it no longer works. Even if certain ministers continue to approach the Ten Commandments in this way, they are merely beating the air, because today this argument is falling on deaf ears.

But the subject can be approached from a different direction.

I will attempt to approach the Ten Commandments *from man's end.* It seems to me that the Ten Commandments themselves give us the right to choose this approach. Let me justify this belief by a simple placement of accents: "*I* am the LORD *your* God"— "Man, the statement concerns *you!* I am *your* God. It is important for you to begin at this point. The subject is you, your life. You have a God." It could have been stated the other way: "Consider, Israel, that you are my people, my possession; therefore beware, mind your slave relationship with me." But God does not remind us that he has a people and that this people had better be careful because he is a hard master. God says, "*You* have a God—I am the LORD your God . . ."

This will be my attempt at a modern procedure—from man's end. And I will set forth at once my main point, and then go on to explain it more fully. If we approach the Ten Commandments from man's end, then the message of the first commandment can be summarized thus: Man, if you really want to become human, *you must have a God. For it is only near God that man becomes human.*

I believe that this is the positive message of the first commandment and that it has something exciting and significant to say to modern man. Man, surely you would like to become fully human? If so you must have a God, because only near him, in relation to him, in conversation with him, can you achieve it. Becoming human means becoming responsive, indeed responsible, to God. This is a difficult assignment. It is easy to understand why a majority of men do not accept it; that then having forsaken the true and living God, other gods, strange gods, come on the scene, and man becomes their slave. This is the modern life we see before us: one runs after cars, another after applause, another after money, or love, or liquor. Everyone has some kind of a god, though it may not be the one true and living God.

In other words we are trying to find a cheaper, easier solution to the problem of life. Instead of the one true God who would ennoble us by having us walk a hard, strenuous path, we choose cheaper, more pleasant, more lenient deities. But every man has some god, some idol whom he serves. In this connection, I repeat, the essence of the first commandment is: If you want to become truly human *you must have this God.* You must bow down before the one living God, because only thus can you become fully man.

I'd like to illustrate my thought in a somewhat unusual manner. I would like to quote a portion from a small contemporary book. The selection offers, I believe, a graphic illustration of the thesis that one cannot become human unless he takes this God.

The book is entitled *You Were a Prophet, My Love,* and it appeared in Hungarian in 1965. The action takes place in a mental health clinic. In four sessions, four persons tell the story of their lives to the psychiatrist. Their stories are uncannily lifelike, with their jumbled thinking, their pitiless honesty, and particularly, their absolute frustration. Let me read just a little bit of the first story. You will see how it illustrates my thesis that without God, you cannot become truly human.

"Honestly, it seems funny that I should be here. What should a gay blade like me be doing in a psychiatrist's office? One always assumes that a libertine has no nerves. But you know better: you know that libertines have nerves, and badly mauled nerves at that. . . . Please, don't rummage in my soul. Once I get going, it won't be necessary for you to interrupt with questions. And I'll be so honest, chum, that I'll have you thinking I'm brilliant. If you wish, I might proceed step by step from where the trouble began. Well, I was a kind of prophet. A popular prophet. Tomorrow we shall turn the whole world upside down! You know the kind, don't you? And what a movement it was, my friend! What a movement! But let's not talk about politics. I don't want to blame my sins on politics. But the truth is, I was not alone as a prophet. A number of us were prophesying, with the sweat dripping from our backs. But then, all at once, I turned around—and now listen carefully, doctor—I still burst out laughing whenever I think of the sight. Imagine, all the prophets around me had grown fat! Did you ever see a fat prophet? A disgusting sight. Their bodies like blubber, their eyes hollow, their mouths like tombs. I admit I was a naive youth then. I was dumfounded. But I was teachable, doctor! I realized that I had to give up such popular fixed ideas as saving the world. I did run head on into the wall a few more times, but then I became quite tame, and I said to myself 'Stop knocking yourself out! If you keep going like this, you'll come to a bad end. And you're not the tragic type!' Life is precious, freedom has to be won wisely each day. Let this day be a good day—let me feel good today; that is what is important, doctor! All kinds of people live that way, in good health, indeed in fatness, at peace with themselves. So, for a while, all went very well. No, you are wrong, I wasn't drinking yet. And my heart was ticking like a Swiss watch. There was only one problem. My wife, she kept buzzing in my ear, 'You were a prophet, my love, and you were beautiful in your prophet days!' "

Enough quoting. Let me tell you the rest. What is this novel about? A gifted young writer tries to be a prophet. He has a vision: Let's go and turn the world upside down! He begins to struggle bravely to make his vision come true. "I was a prophet and there were other prophets around me. But suddenly I saw that the prophets were getting fat. They were getting into their Volga automobiles. Their bank deposits were increasing. Then I had to start thinking: Listen, be smart! They are being smart!"

So the young writer also gives up prophecy. But there is one disturbing element, his wife, who keeps telling him how much she used to admire him when he was a prophet. This disturbs him. He's angry at his wife, he fights her, he resists her. At last he lets her go, children and all; indeed he practically hounds them out of their home. Then he creates for himself a new philosophy of life, the philosophy of the prophet turned traitor. And then he makes the ghastly confession, "I could not endure my philosophy. This is what brought me to the mental health clinic."

Well put. He had a prophet's vision, which he betrayed. From his betrayal he created a philosophy which then he could not stand because something inside him kept saying, "This is all a lie." So he landed in the mental health clinic. There he tells his story which ends in his collapse. Now let the needles come and the shock treatment, for this is no life.

Let us analyze the situation. This man nearly became human. If I were a critic I would add another word to the title of the book: *Almost.* "Almost you were a prophet, my love." This man made a start on Jeremiah's road. He had visions. He saw things that needed destroying and others that needed building. He set out on the road with a prophet's vision. Then came the struggles. He fought a good fight. But after a while he looked at his fellow prophets and saw that they were getting fat. This was the decisive moment of his life. Listen carefully, because even here the Word of God has something for us. When he reached the point where he still knew that his visions were true but that the prophets around him were getting fat, he asked himself why he should remain a lean prophet. And this was the decisive moment of his life. He could not hold on to his vision. He began to "adjust." This was his tragedy! That he had no God to confirm him in his vision. He had no God, and therefore he could not become a man. This is a hard thing to say, but I'm convinced that it is true. This striking novel says the same thing in its own negative way. He did not know God, who could have helped him, who could have strengthened him against the faithlessness of the fat prophets, who could have fortified him in his hard fight. *Therefore* he could not become a man. And in the end he was punished for his sin by being unable to endure his own philosophy. He did not know God, he created a philosophy for himself, but it would not do. The whole structure caved in. He could not become human.

Now, in contrast with the fate of this caved-in prophet, let us recall Jeremiah once more. It all began the same way with him. God spoke to him and gave him a vision and a task. Then Jeremiah became mindful of the difficulties and he was frightened. But God said to him, "Don't be frightened. I am with you." These few words, "I am with you," are the secret of Jeremiah's destiny as a prophet, of Jeremiah's humanity. Every man has something like a prophet's mission, at least in the simple sense of the term that sooner or later he beholds a vision, he becomes aware of his mission in life: "I will be a teacher. I will be a physician. I will be a minister, or a worker, or a labor leader." Then he sees all around him the fat teachers, the fat doctors, the fat clergymen. And he says to himself, "Why should I be different?" And this is the point at which it will be decided whether or not he will become a man. The moment the dreadful question arises, "Why should I be unlike the others?"—that very moment his humanity is being decided upon. For at some time or another each one of us receives the order: Be different, be unlike the others! It is this "un-likeness" we must demonstrate in the office, in the kitchen, the shop, the pulpit. And each one of us has this mission. This is the way to break out of the crowd. This is the way to become truly human—to become unlike the others.

But this is not easy; the crowd does not tolerate difference. It makes short shrift of anyone who does not conform. This is the secret of becoming human. And woe to him who looks at the others, who pays attention to the fat prophets, who has no God. The struggle of becoming human can be endured only if we have a God —*this* God. "Do not be dismayed by them, lest I dismay you before them" (Jer. 1:17, R.S.V.). This is what God said to the young Jeremiah—that if he got away from him, from God, everything would dismay him!

This then is my interpretation of the Ten Commandments: "I am the LORD your God . . . You shall have no other gods before me." I put it, positively, thus: "Man, it is your mission to become human. But to accomplish this mission, you need me. Without me it does not work, because to become human means to see a vision, to hold on to the vision faithfully, to receive strength from above, and to keep going, through the whole crowd of false prophets, straight ahead on the path which I have appointed." He who does this is human. The rest are herd.

We stand before God; we are measured with God's measure. The writer of the novel had some understanding of what it would mean to be a prophet. But the hero of his novel failed at the task. It all came to an end in the office of the psychiatrist. And I believe that the writer is correct. Without God, that is the last stop. That, or shoddy compromise—a few inches of fat around the midriff, a few feet of fat around the brain!

A few more words about "You shall have no other gods before me." The way it happens is not that man forsakes the one true God and *chooses* for himself a strange god. It is rather that when we fall from the love of one true God, we fall prey to strange gods. We land in the clutches of strange gods. The novel which we have been discussing is interesting to examine from this point of view, too: How and to whom did the hero fall prey?

His philosophy, the one he used to justify his faithlessness, is dreadful indeed. He knows that his philosophy is shoddy, stupid, that he is a cynic. He also knows that those who are successful are dunderheads. And now he is trying to comfort himself with the knowledge, "At least I have not been deceived." But then he falls prey to the idol alcohol, he surrenders to its mindless rapture, because it offers some consolation, some new visions. And if that is not enough, there is sex. At least, sex stirs the nerves a little and gives the illusion of being alive. His wife, who reminds and prods him, has become unbearable to him. His whole life collapses. The description is vivid, perhaps even exaggerated, but I say that it is the story of a great many men. He who loses the one true God falls prey to strange gods—money, power, drugs, sex. They cast their spell upon him and hold him captive so that he can no longer become human.

To summarize: We are looking at the first commandment, "I am the LORD your God . . . You shall have no other gods before me," in a modern perspective. It is not telling us to go to church diligently or be damned. It would be a terrible thing, to have such a primitive view of the first commandment! No, the first commandment says, "Man, if you want to become human, if you want to become a little different from the crowd, then you need God. For if God is not holding you up, you are swept away and you become inhuman."

Do you understand? It is not possible to lead a fully human life in the office, in the family circle, in the world at large, without God. This is the positive aspect of the first commandment: Man, if you want to become human, accept God's outstretched hand. Accept it and grasp it, for to become human you must walk hand-in-hand with him.

In the Bible, God's outstretched hand is Jesus Christ. It is through him that God approaches us, draws near to us, grasps our hand. Jesus Christ is the God-given help by which we can become human. He is *Man*—which is what Pilate noted in that remarkable prophetic insight which somehow surfaced from his superficiality, *ecce homo*! Jesus Christ is God's outstretched hand, with whose help we can become human.

Jesus Christ helps us to become human in four different ways.

1. In Jesus Christ, in his nearness and purity, we recognize our mission, the prophetic service which we must render. God shows us our mission through Christ.

2. It is through Christ that God gives us the power to accomplish our mission. "I can do all things in him who strengthens me" (R.S.V.).

3. And when we're not doing well in this business of becoming human—and we must admit that time and again we are not doing well at all—it is through Christ that God offers comfort and wisdom and forgiveness.

4. And, finally, God gives us hope through Christ. Now things are not going well, but they will! In this life things do not run smoothly, but in the life everlasting they will! It is through Jesus Christ that we become human. It is through Jesus Christ that we understand the first commandment, "I am the LORD your God—seek me, cling to me, stay near me, for only thus can you lead a human life. Cling to me through Jesus Christ, and don't become enslaved to any other gods, because they will ruin you, they will trample your humanity underfoot. Near me, you will become truly man."

# II

# YOU SHALL NOT MAKE
# FOR YOURSELF
# A GRAVEN IMAGE

EXODUS 20:4–6

"You shall not make for yourself a graven image . . ." (R.S.V.).

I understand that in Israel, in Jerusalem, tourists keep trying in vain to snap pictures of Orthodox Jews. These cloaked, bearded people offer superb subjects for photographs as they walk the narrow streets of their city, talking and arguing with each other. But as soon as they notice the lens of a camera trained on them, they draw the cloak over their face. This is how strictly they observe the commandment "You shall not make for yourself a graven image." The making of all images is forbidden: not only of God (be it a statue or a painting) but of man as well. For thousands of years the commandment has been ingrained in the Jewish people: Images are forbidden.

Are they exaggerating? Are they misunderstanding the law? I suggest that we do not make a hasty judgment in the matter. For the moment let us simply note that these people have been dramatizing an idea for thousands of years and that they are still dramatizing it. First, then, let us discover the idea itself. Then we will have an opportunity to determine whether this idea—which is undoubtedly a divine revelation—needs to be interpreted this way in our time. And whatever our answer may prove to be, our primary concern must not be a matter of conduct but the idea, the divine truth voiced in the text "You shall not make for yourself a graven image."

Why does God not want us to make any images of him? How does it *hurt* God if we thus picture him? A strange question. How can we imagine what may hurt God? For, evidently, it is hurting him to be represented by an image. If we could fathom the reasons for his pain, we would understand his reasons for forbidding the making of images. But is it possible to understand the pain of God?

Let me hazard the bold thesis that it is possible to understand God's pain. It is possible to experience his pain just a little. And to the extent that we can experience his pain within the small sphere of our life, we will understand the intent of this divine commandment. I have myself experienced something of God's pain and, if you pay close attention, you will realize that you, too, have experienced it. Let me illustrate.

Some time ago I was at a large party, surrounded by strangers. Whatever the conversation was about, eventually it turned to God. What did we think of God? They all turned to me. They wanted me to speak. And then one of the guests said, "Well, of course, you are a minister. You can speak to this point in your official capacity!"

What does this mean? It means that this man had made for himself an image of a minister, a graven image—not of stone or of wood, but of thought. He had made himself a clear, firm likeness. He had constructed a pigeonhole and put me in it. Whatever I might say, I would have to say it from the pigeonhole labeled "minister."

I felt extremely rebellious: "This simply isn't right!" To be sure, I am a clergyman by profession, but I may just be able to say something in my own right. I experienced the pigeonholing as an injustice. It hurt to be treated not like a man, an individual, but like a statue, like a picture stored in a case. There is something painful about this experience. And this is why God experiences pain when we give him the rigid, fixed likeness of a "graven image."

There are many other examples. For instance, we say, "Of course—you're a woman." "Of course—you are Jewish." We have come to expect certain attitudes, certain responses, of women or of Jews, and at once we put any woman, or any Jew, in a suitable box. People constantly work with pigeonholes. They go on and on making graven images. And this is grossly unjust, because human beings are not the stereotypes they are alleged to be.

Of course, this making of images—of stereotypes—is entirely natural and understandable. It is difficult to treat every person as an individual. So we engage in reduction, in simplification. We make up categories such as "women"—and thereafter we expect every individual woman to fit. Or "atheist"—and at once we feel that we have mastered a reality with a million faces. We make boxes, I say, and we work with them.

Thus the Orthodox Jews in their cloaks are right when they insist that the commandment "You shall not make for yourself a graven image" does not apply only to God, but to man as well. It means that you must not get off lightly, cheaply, by taking a few pictures, a few clichés, so that by trapping people in them you will think you own the world. If you have the whole world in pictures —in pictures which you possess—the world becomes simple, and you are lord over that world.

Within the urge to make pictures—whether the old, primitive way, out of wood or stone, or, in a more complicated contemporary fashion, out of thought—hides the desire to get the upper hand over what is portrayed, to rule over the subject pictured. The history of religion demonstrates clearly that the reason for making likenesses of God was that in this way people thought to dominate their gods. Of course, they also worshiped them and sacrificed to them. They would wash them, dress them, symbolically feed them, perform a variety of rituals for them, and bow down before them. But what really mattered was that in this way they were, in effect, achieving mastery over the gods: "Look, God, I'm feeding you, I'm paying you homage, but in exchange you must do *my* will."

But this is what God does not permit. He will not stand for it, whether it is done in a primitive form, as among the pagans, or in more sophisticated forms, as we Christians use. For we too have our images of God and, under the guise of service to our God-image, we try to force God into our service. But God does not allow it. Rather, he cuts off the very attempt at its root when he says, "You shall not make for yourself a graven image."

In the Old Testament there is a scene in the time of the high priest Eli, when the Jews had become mixed up in a war with the Philistines. They had lost the first battle. They had become discouraged. What next? Then it occurred to them that they might take the ark of the covenant into their camp. An interesting thought. They were not permitted to make graven images but there was the ark of the covenant which nevertheless represented the presence of God in some fashion. "We are losing, so let's go and take the ark to the battlefield. Then God will be there and we'll be sure to win the next battle."

The Bible then describes how they carried the ark to their camp —and proceeded to lose the next battle as well. God did not oblige. God had a quarrel with his people, and this quarrel could not be resolved so lightly, so cheaply. A mere magical trick was not enough. Indeed, God permitted the ark to be captured by the Philistines and to be placed next to the statue of their god, Dagon. He permitted this because he wanted to teach his people that they could not manipulate him in this way, least of all by the kind of magic which is supposed to inhere in a painting or a statue where one can light a candle and then everything will be all right because one has mobilized the heavenly powers.

Let's be quite clear on this point: Either God mobilizes me in the sense that I submit to his holy will, or else I succeed in mobilizing him so that he will help carry out my purposes. This is the everlasting struggle in the history of religion—can man mobilize God or can God mobilize man? And Christianity is unique among the religions of mankind in that Christians radically reject putting God at the service of their aims. The Christian faith is a faith in which our human will is surrendered in the conviction that God's will is better. We submit to God's will so that he may lead or carry us wherever he will. This is the claim stated in the second commandment. God will not have us mobilize him, but he will bear us up and guide us. "You shall not make for yourself a graven image." God will not have us get the upper hand over him by means of any statue, picture, art, or whatever likeness we may devise. He will not have us lead him around. To become a Christian means to give up trying to lord it over him, and to let him become our lord.

To go on to the positive message of the commandment: God

has revealed himself in Jesus Christ. There is only one trustworthy likeness of God and that is the likeness we have in Jesus Christ. Of course, we are not talking about the many beautiful paintings in which his life and suffering are portrayed. We are talking rather about God's self-disclosure in Jesus Christ as a continuously moving self-disclosure. For wherever Jesus went he created a new situation. He was utterly unpredictable. He would not be possessed by anyone, nor could he be bought off. Rather he invited submission.

In Jesus, God disclosed himself as the fountain of compassion, so that the only possible response is to kneel before him and to adore him. In Jesus, God revealed himself as the friend of sinners, as the good shepherd who goes in search of the lost sheep. Such is God. But we cannot take advantage of God's compassion by deciding to become the one-hundredth, the lost sheep, in order that God may come looking for us! For the same Jesus picked up a whip against the money changers who were treating God as their private property. If we would meet God, we can meet him in Jesus Christ. But even then, we can meet him only on our knees, in self-surrender to him, and never in a way that would indicate that we had, thanks to Jesus, at last taken possession of God.

I think we can sum up the essence of the second commandment in this way: "I am the Lord your God; don't try to capture me. Rather, let yourself be captured by me, since you see that I am a great and mighty God. You shall not make for yourself a graven image!"

The other aspect of our theme concerns not God but man. I believe that the Jews in Jerusalem are right not to permit pictures to be taken of men, either. Not in the primitive sense, of course, which seems to make photography a sin, but in the spiritual sense, in which we are warned against putting people into pigeonholes.

This is the way we usually operate. We have a fixed image of our children, of our husbands, of our wives, of our clergy, of our enemies. According to our faith, this is wrong. The second commandment implies that we must not make graven images of people either, because there is more to any person than can be captured in any image, no matter how good the likeness is. Of course parents know their children. But I have a growing suspicion that the child

they think they know, whose picture lives in their mind, is no longer
the same child. Parents cannot keep up with the passage of time.
The child has changed. It has been a long time since he was the
child whose picture the parents have fixed in their minds. And the
same applies to the husband-wife relationship. It takes time to make
an image, to develop a picture, and by the time it is finished, the
person has changed. "You shall not make for yourself a graven
image." Don't believe in your images; reality is very different.

But we must look into the matter more deeply. It is not just that
we are making mistakes because reality has changed while we have
been holding on to a fixed, a dramatic, image of either God or man.
Modern psychology and a number of modern writers agree that
these stereotypes are *harmful.* They hurt the other party as well.
Max Frisch has a little story about a young man from Andorra
about whom the rumor had begun to spread that he was really
Jewish. So people projected upon him the stereotyped notion that
he was doing everything just for money! They began to suspect
him. In the end he himself became confused: "Who am I? They say
I'm doing everything only for money." In the end he believed the
accusation himself, so strongly had the stereotype been projected
upon him. He could no longer defend himself against it because it
had penetrated his subconscious. They hated him more and more.
In the end they attacked and killed him. Then, of course, it came
to light that he had been a native of Andorra, like all the rest, and
that there was not a grain of truth to the rumor. By pigeonholing
him, they had created a situation in which he could not be himself.
They had put him in a box from which he could not break out. A
fearful story. And it is a novelist, not a theologian, who illustrates
the commandment "You shall not make for yourself a graven
image."

I remember a saying of Jean-Paul Sartre. He was asked what
*I* means. Who is *I*? His response was brief but intensely interesting:
"My freedom—that is I." In other words, I have inherited my body,
my character, and all sorts of other things from my parents, but
I myself am this—my freedom. The color of my eyes was deter-
mined by the color of my grandparents' eyes, of my parents' eyes.
But this is not I. I am my freedom. I am he who does something

with all his inheritance. I rebel against my inheritance. Or I acquiesce in my inheritance. A profound statement! "My freedom—that is I." I am he who, in some way, comes to grips with this inheritance. I am the movement, the struggle, the rebellion against my inheritance!

Thus we see the truth of the second commandment as it applies to man, in that whoever makes himself a fixed image of a person deprives that person of his possibility, of his freedom. The person is trapped in a particular likeness: "This is you! I knew your father and your mother. I know what to expect of you." Thus what the man is not is fixed forever, and he is robbed of what he is. In other words, by making such a likeness of a man, I trap him in what he was yesterday or in what he might be today, and I make it impossible for him to develop freely into what he may become tomorrow. This applies to the husband-wife relationship, to the teacher-student relationship. I make myself an image. "I knew your father; you will be a liar too," says the professor. The possibility that the child will be a liar increases.

This is a fearfully concrete problem if we lift it above its religious generality and behold it in the depths of its lifelike truth. God will not have us bind him to whatever knowledge of him we possessed yesterday! And this applies not only to words but to entire systems of doctrine. The fact that we came to know God yesterday or the day before in a certain way does not mean that he can be bound, that he can be held to that form, that he will always act in that way: "Man, I'm not putting my freedom at your disposal."

And God is saying the same thing in man's behalf as well. "You shall not make for yourself a graven image" of any human being, because such a fixed image robs him of his freedom. So don't make yourself any such likenesses of anyone, but choose the more difficult task. Say, "I don't know. I will watch you. I want to see what you develop into."

The second commandment is the commandment of freedom. To be sure, all the others are freedom commandments, too. God demands for himself full freedom to act. This is why he does not permit us to make images of him. At the same time he demands full freedom for man. So the idea behind the injunction against the making of images is not that we must not engage in photography. The meaning is far more profound. God demands full freedom for man. We must not fix the essence of any man in a convenient category, a mental snapshot. Honor God's freedom and honor each other's freedom as well!

To carry the thought to a still deeper level: It occurs to me that whoever fabricates such images eventually becomes an image himself. Remember how God delivered Lot and his family from Sodom but how he could not tear Lot's wife away from the city? God had forbidden them to look back. But Lot's wife could not resist taking that last picture of Sodom so that she might carry it away in her heart—a picture of the beloved, beautiful city! But God had forbidden it: "You shall not make for yourself a graven image" of Sodom. But Lot's wife could not resist the temptation. She turned around, stared like a camera with a wide lens, and turned into a pillar of salt! The mythical element does not matter; it is the profound truth that counts. Whoever insists on making pictures and does not allow reality to develop freely turns into a graven image himself. The second commandment is remarkably concrete.

I'd like to close by referring once more to Max Frisch's story about the young man from Andorra. All of us are forever dealing with the injustice that comes to man as a result of fixed, rigid images. We inflict the damage on others and are in turn damaged by others except—except—if we *love one another*. If we love one another, we stop dealing in stereotypes with one another. Love offers freedom of movement, freedom for change and growth. Love respects the other person. As long as we deal in stereotypes, we are actually trying to dominate one another. But love enables us to set each other free. As Max Frisch says, "Others are forever sinning against us and we against them, unless we love one another."

And this, in turn, applies just as much to our relationship with God. If you love God, you will give him a free hand. If you truly love God you will be able to say to him, "Even if you damn me, you are right, and if you save me, I adore you."

To love God means that we do not attempt to tie God's hands in order to make use of him for our purposes. If we love God, we give him a free hand. If we truly worship God, we will pay homage to him *today* and then keep our eyes open to see how he will be acting tomorrow. This is the way to be a child of God! "I know that you are God, the Father of Jesus Christ, and I know that tomorrow again you will give me some fresh and wondrous token of your patience and love. I am waiting for your tomorrow. What will it bring?"

He who does give God a free hand really loves God. And he who does give man his freedom truly loves man: "True, yesterday you slapped my face, you were miserable to me, but today you will be different. I will not allow myself to be bound by yesterday's performance. I am looking for what you are today, for the way you approach me today."

He who loves man grants this freedom to any man, that he may begin anew today; and only he who grants such freedom to his fellowmen, is truly a lover of men.

May God give us strength truly to demolish all graven images. Let us destroy our dogmatic likenesses of God and come before him like children, saying, "I don't know what you will do next, but I trust you because I have begun to come to know you in Jesus Christ."

And let us destroy our fixed likenesses of one another and grant one another freedom to change. If many memories have accumulated, they are not valid, they do not count. You are a man, a free man. I want to meet you today in freedom, without prejudice. This is a life worth living. This is God's design for our worship of him as well as for our relations with one another. Let us fit into this design, no longer making images, throwing out the stereotypes and all other shortcuts, and resolving to meet the real God as well as our real fellowmen on this steep but far more satisfying path.

# III

## YOU SHALL NOT TAKE
## THE NAME OF THE LORD
## YOUR GOD IN VAIN

### Exodus 20:7

"You shall not take the name of the LORD your God in vain; for the LORD will not hold him guiltless who takes his name in vain" (R.S.V.).

As a child, preparing for my confirmation, I learned that people were breaking the third commandment primarily in two ways: by swearing nastily or by taking oaths or vows flippantly. In those days hardly anyone swore except cabdrivers and drill sergeants. These would not normally be churchgoing people; therefore, it was possible to point a finger at them through the church window as if to say, "See, those are the people who break the commandment!" As for the use of oaths, it was a practice limited largely to gypsies and Jews: "May I never again see my blessed mother!" "Let God strike me down!" "I swear on the very life of my children!" Naturally, they were not churchgoing people either. Thus it was possible to do with this commandment what we are so apt to do with all the commandments, namely, for the good church people to say, "Look, *they* are the ones who are breaking the third commandment! I thank thee, God, that I am not like them! I'm here in thy church, offering proper homage to thee!"

This was the perspective in which I came to know the Ten Commandments as a child. This is how they were taught to us in our confirmation instruction and this was the way the entire congregation, by and large, viewed them. But it should be obvious that today my view of the Ten Commandments in general and of the third commandment in particular is quite different. Specifically, I interpret the message of the third commandment as a message addressed primarily to the congregation of believers. For it is my conviction that this commandment is directed primarily at us praying, preaching, witnessing, churchly people.

In interpreting this commandment, let us first of all recall an important biblical truth about the meaning of *names*. In ancient times, names had enormous significance. This is something we have largely forgotten. Today naming has become an esthetic problem. Parents and godparents choose among names in order to present the child with one that sounds nice, and with that, the task is concluded. But in the ancient world matters were different. People used to believe that a name signified the very essence of something or someone. Whoever knew the name of a thing or a person possessed in a sense the thing or person whose name he knew. Knowledge of the name gave a man power over the person or thing.

Let us recall some appropriate material from the Bible. In the creation story we read that God lined up all the animals before man, and man gave them names. According to ancient, mythical thinking, this meant that man took possession of the animals one by one, and began to rule over them. This power was signified by the giving of names.

When parents named a child, they would pour their faith, their hope, their prophetic vision—if there was such—into the name, so that the name was placed upon the child as a token of his destiny. Remember how the prophet Hosea chose names for his children so that, by their names, they would bear a message concerning the destiny of Israel, a message addressed by God to his people.

Recognizing and understanding the name of God was especially important. Let us recall the scene at the burning bush when God speaks to Moses and orders him to go among his brothers in order to deliver them from their enslavement in Egypt. Moses replies, "All right, I will go, but if they ask me who has sent me, what shall I say? What is your name?" Moses wants to know God's name not only because he wants to know God, but also because, by knowing

God's name, he may achieve a little mastery over God; by using his name, he might call upon God. Moses is very much disturbed about this business of God's name. He will not go until he finds out. Then follows that marvelous self-revealing in which God both says something about himself and does not say anything.

He tells Moses, "Say this to the people of Israel, 'I AM has sent me to you'" (R.S.V.). This "I AM" is expressed by five Hebrew letters, YAHWEH, a mysterious Hebrew word that stands for the concept of being. "Say that 'I AM,' *the one who truly exists*, has sent me to you who live like shadows, who live a life derived from my life."

"I AM WHO I AM," says God—at least this is an acceptable translation. Jewish and Christian scholars have been disputing for centuries the exact meaning of this baffling divine self-disclosure. Nowadays Old Testament scholars say that a better translation might be, "I am who I am becoming." This means that you cannot get to know God unless and until you are *on the march*. You will get to know him from those experiences which you will acquire while walking with him. Thus God is saying something, but he is not delivering himself altogether to Moses. And from that day forward, this sacred name will lead the Jews and will become their great treasure. This is the mysterious name of which the commandment says, "You shall not take the name of the LORD your God in vain."

Now to say something about changes of names—another very interesting subject: The Bible has many stories about how someone received one name from his family and afterward another—how God himself changed his name or how it was changed for some other reason. In ancient times, a change of name signified that a man was lifted out of his old setting and brought under the influence of new forces in a new context. This was so even in the pagan world. We read in the book of Daniel that Daniel and his three friends were taken to Babylon and there were given new names, Babylonian names. What this means is that they were taken out of their Jewish rootage, loyalty, religion, so that they might be assimilated into Babylonian culture. This would be the consequence of the change of names.

We lived through a startling new version of this ancient practice in the days when Hitler and company acted out their revolt against the Bible by making it virtually mandatory for people to give their children old German names. They too were reckoning with the mysterious power of names. They were quite aware of the fact that as long as German children had Christian names they would be susceptible to Christian influences. Thus, the giving of new names was part of the rebellion against Christianity, as well as an attempt to mobilize ancient pagan powers.

But this is what the Christians had been doing in the early days of the church. All baptized persons were given new names—biblical names instead of their pagan names. Saint Augustine's son was baptized *Adeodatus,* which meant *given by God.* In this way the early Christians expressed their intention to extricate the baptized person from the net of ancient pagan powers and to bring him under Christian influence. A name then signified possession, power. And saying someone's name meant in effect calling upon him, mobilizing him.

When the disciples returned from their first mission, they announced joyfully to Jesus, "Lord, even the demons are subject to us in your name!" (R.S.V.). They would say, "In the name of Jesus of Nazareth," and power flowed. When the beggar at the gate asked Peter and John to be healed, Peter said to him, "I have no silver and gold, but I give you what I have; in the name of Jesus of Nazareth, walk" (R.S.V.). Pronouncing the name of Jesus of Nazareth amounted to marshaling his power. As soon as his name was pronounced, the sick would rise and be healed. And when a great commotion arose as a result of some of these healings, the apostles testified that the miracles had occurred not as a result of any of their doing or strength but as a result of the name upon which they had called.

There is a great deal of beautiful theology in the Scripture that has to do with names. It would be worthwhile to review the entire Bible from this standpoint. Here I would merely like to quote the text that, more than any other, has warmed my heart as I study the Scripture. It is the text which contains Aaron's blessing (Num. 6:22-27).

The LORD said to Moses, "Say to Aaron and his sons, Thus you shall bless the people of Israel: you shall say to them,

The LORD bless you and keep you:
The LORD make his face to shine
  upon you, and be gracious to you:
The LORD lift up his countenance
  upon you, and give you peace.

"So shall they put my name upon the people of Israel, and I will bless them" (R.S.V.).

Just observe how marvelous this simple statement is, what spiritual riches are contained in the sentence, "So shall they put my name upon the people of Israel, and I will bless them." God's name is to be placed upon the children of Israel as a *blessing*. This proves again that a name is far more than an esthetic phenomenon, a matter of sound that we utter with no particular results. According to the belief of people in ancient times, a name was a summons, a mobilization of forces. "Put my name upon your people" meant, "Put the knowledge of me, put my divine blessing, put the strength of my presence, upon your people." If we want to enter into the spirit of the Bible, we have to learn that names are not idle sounds, but rather summonses of power.

Let me offer a perhaps inept but moving comparison. A soldier is wounded in the battlefield. Collapsing with pain, he cries out "Mother!" And perhaps thousands of miles away his mother clasps her heart and cries out, "My son!" and this is happening at the very moment when the young man, in pain, has cried out! In some mysterious way, by some strange, unknown process of shortwave communication or whatever it may be, the son's cry reaches the mother, who knows that something has happened. But she is helpless. She can only clasp her heart; she can do nothing to help her son. However, the story shows the connection between a name and calling upon, mobilizing, a person, even though the mother in this case cannot help.

But in the case of God it is a different matter. Whenever anyone cries out in the midst of suffering or misery, "O God, my Father, have mercy on me!" there is no idle stirring of the airwaves. There is a mobilization. And it is directed toward that God who is present, who is full of compassion, who has pity, who wants to help. This is the crux of the matter: To use the name of God is to call upon him, to summon him.

As another biblical illustration of the power of a name, let us remember the scene in which Elijah is struggling with the priests of Baal on Mount Carmel. The priests are building an altar and shouting, "O Baal, answer us!" But their shouting is in vain because Baal is powerless. Then it is Elijah's turn. He, too, is building an altar and then he begins to pray: "O LORD, God of Abraham, Isaac, and Israel, let it be known this day that thou art God in Israel . . ." (R.S.V.). Elijah also is calling upon the name of his God, and we know what happens: a great fire bursts out; God has accepted Elijah's sacrifice. For the use of God's name is not merely a psychological gesture, something to relieve one's spirits, but it signifies a genuine mobilization in the spiritual realm, with startling consequences. With this interpretation in mind then, we will no longer be surprised when the third commandment says to us, "Don't do it. Don't rush. Don't repeat yourself."

But the matter is not as simple as that. "You shall not take the name of the LORD your God in vain." This "in vain" is not a good phrase. The original says "unworthily," "improperly." The German translation, *missbrauchen*, means to misuse, to abuse. Do not abuse the name of God! The essence of the commandment is that there is in the name of God a fearful power; be careful not to abuse it! And the reason given in the Old Testament is this: "for the LORD will not hold him guiltless who takes his name in vain."

And now we have arrived at the essential question. Who is using the name of God unworthily? How is it possible to take advantage of God's name? What is the greatest of sins according to the Bible? The greatest of sins is the sin of violence, the sin of aggressiveness. If we read the Bible correctly, it becomes clear that the cardinal sin is for man to play God, as if he were lord of the living and of the dead. If violence is the cardinal sin, then to take the name of God in vain or unworthily or wickedly means to do violence to God. This is what we do whenever we use his name to magical ends of our own, to help us accomplish our will. No matter how devoutly a man says his prayers, he is using prayer wickedly if in his heart he is saying, "You are in my power, God. I know you. I'm holding your promises in my hand. God, let *my* will be done! Now do what I'm asking you!"

We are even more likely to be aggressive with God's name toward our fellowmen. Whenever we attempt to dominate our fellowmen and use the name of God to buttress our claim upon them, we are in effect breaking the third commandment. When human beings are burned at the stake in the name of God—when a pope excommunicates a Luther *"in nomine Dei"*—the commandment is being broken dreadfully. The rude curses of cabdrivers are offensive, but far more offensive is a high priest who in the name of God puts a curse upon another in whom the Holy Spirit dwells more fully than it does in the high priest! This is violence committed in the name of faith. "You are threatening my supremacy; therefore, in the name of God, be cursed!" Can there be a more dreadful abuse of the name of God? Will God leave us unpunished when we try to sanctify and legitimate our own greed for power in his name? This is the cardinal sin. When we use God's name for our own selfish ends, that is sin writ large.

And here we have to mention the case of the church allowing itself to be pressed into the service of such aggression. It is a sad truth that this is happening in our own time. I have in mind instances when the church itself is not aggressive but legitimates the violence of others in the name of God. For example, when the church blesses weapons of war and prays for the victory of the army, that it may massacre as many of the enemy soldiers as possible, this too is taking the name of God in vain.

I have lived through many terrible experiences, but one of the most awful things I remember occurred toward the end of 1944 when suddenly little slips of paper appeared among us with the message, "We shall be Christ's whip!" (Some of you no doubt remember them.) This, of course, was directed at the Jews and at anyone who would not embrace the Nazi ideology. "We shall be Christ's whip." The Nazis were usurping God's name. But when the church legitimated this claim, when the church supported the mass murder of the Jews by saying, "God's judgment is upon them;

they have deserved it," this is of all the abuses of God's name the most horrifying! And it haunts us to this day. Perhaps the church is no longer tempted to burn people at the stake. Its power to do so has been taken away. But the aggressive powers of this world still need the church's amens to bless their deeds of bloody violence.

Just a few days ago I heard that the renowned evangelist Billy Graham, whose name also shines in Europe, is supposed to have said that we should rally to the defense of Christianity by carrying on a crusade in Vietnam. And he is apparently enlisting followers in this cause. My friends, this is dreadful! When a Christian evangelist speaks of bombings and mass murder as a "crusade" for the defense of Christian civilization, we are in the presence of a grievous transgression against the commandment "You shall not take the name of the Lord in vain." The least the evangelist could do would be to say, "Our Christianity is impotent; we don't understand what is going on in the world; we have no word from the Lord." But let him not set forth his own philosophy as if it were the word of God! Billy Graham could have said, "I don't understand what is going on in the world"; and believe me, this might frequently be the most honest form of Christian witness—to admit that we do not know what God wants nor what we must do. This would be a thousand times better than to say, "Thus says the Lord, 'Drop your bombs on them!'"

This is my conviction, and I believe that I have some understanding of God's Word. Christianity would be hurt less if we were willing to say with respect to any of the world's problems, "I do not know," rather than to claim divine sanction for Eastern thinking in the East and for Western thinking in the West so that both sides take God's name in vain. How much better it would be if Christians on both sides wept and confessed that what is going on in the world exceeds their spiritual capacities and that they have no prophet, no word from the Lord. At least we would be keeping silent; and we would weep, we would mourn those who were being massacred. Do you understand how contemporary this commandment is?

One further thought in closing: I believe that Jesus lifts us well above the level of the Old Testament world. He is saying more to us than just the Ten Commandments. When it comes to the reason why we should not unworthily, flippantly, use the name of God, the Old Testament tells us that "the LORD will not hold him guiltless who takes his name in vain." This is the atmosphere of the Old Covenant: to fear, to dread. And indeed, pious Jews would not utter the name *Yahweh*. They laboriously circumscribed it. The atmosphere of the Old Covenant is an atmosphere of fear: "Don't do it, for God will not let you go unpunished."

But Jesus takes us on a better path. He first brings to us God's new name. What is this wonderful, simple new name which stands forth as a unique and amazing phenomenon in the history of religion? It is the name *Father*. Dear Father, good Father—this is how Jesus taught us to address God. He brought God as near to us as a father is near. He encouraged us to speak to God in an atmosphere of trust. And when Jesus affirms the third commandment, he does not say that we should not talk much about God because he will punish us; rather he says, "When you pray, go into a quiet room and there pray quietly. And don't talk much to people about God" (see Matthew 6). Jesus retains the essence of the commandment—that we should not spoil God's name with an excess of talk—but the reason he gives is not that God will punish us, but, so far as I am able to understand him, that God may leave us. Communion with God is a wonderful thing. We must not make it into a weapon for ourselves. Nor must we idly chatter about it. It is a sacred thing; therefore, let us not continually use God's name, lest he withdraw from us. The Old Testament thought was, "Don't do it, because God will strike you down." But Jesus says, "God is your heavenly Father. Do not offend him by using his name constantly, routinely, thoughtlessly. Let your communion with him be a holy thing. If you keep using God's name, you may lose touch with him. If you talk about him all the time, your fellowship with him may become an empty thing; indeed it may come to nothing."

It was only in 1965 that the world-renowned Jewish scholar Martin Buber died. He was the greatest Jewish philosopher and Bible scholar of our generation. In commenting upon the scene in which Moses at the burning bush hears the voice of God, "I AM who I am," Buber says that the essence of this revelation is, "I am *here*!" In other words, "I do not need to be summoned, I am here in your midst already!" According to Buber, God's self-disclosure meant, "O my people, don't believe that you have to drag me down from heaven with fear-ridden magic. My very name is 'I am here.' I am here all the time, I am with you at all times." That perhaps is the most profound meaning of the third commandment. Do not summon God all the time, for in so doing you are only demonstrating your own lack of faith.

The reason for our reading the Twenty-third Psalm today was that in this Psalm the same insight appears.

> The Lord is my shepherd, I shall not want;
>     he makes me lie down in green pastures.
> He leads me beside still waters;
>     he restores my soul.
> He leads me in paths of righteousness
>     for his name's sake (R.S.V.).

He's doing all these things not because of my praying, but "for his name's sake." This is what Martin Buber is saying: God has revealed that he is here, that it is not necessary to summon him up by magic. This is the faith for which we must strive. This does not mean that we have to stop praying, but rather that our prayers should glorify God, that they should voice our thanks to God for being present with us. Our prayers should say, "Lord, I have noticed your presence, I trust you, I leave my fate in your hands."

It is possible to use the name of God rightly, but this is something that has to be learned—and God's people are the first who must learn it. May his Holy Spirit help us in this task!

# IV

## THE CHRISTIAN'S WORK AND REST

EXODUS 20:8–11

"Remember the sabbath day, to keep it holy. Six days you shall labor, and do all your work; but the seventh day is a sabbath to the LORD your God; in it you shall not do any work, you, or your son, or your daughter, your manservant, or your maidservant, or your cattle, or the sojourner who is within your gates; for in six days the LORD made heaven and earth, the sea, and all that is in them, and rested the seventh day; therefore the LORD blessed the sabbath day and hallowed it" (R.S.V.).

This commandment really calls for two sermons: one on the call to labor for six days and get all our work done, the other on how we must rest on the seventh day and sanctify that day. The truth is that we have problems on both counts. We are not able either to work or to rest according to God's will. Or to put it more simply, we cannot work soundly and, at the end of six days, we cannot rest soundly, because when man cut himself off from God, he lost the divine order of things and, with it, he lost life. Ever since, there has been no blessing or joy in man's work and no real refreshment in man's rest.

It is my belief that the two parts of this commandment belong together so closely that it is not possible for us to separate them. It is not possible to develop a division of labor whereby, let us say, socialism will teach men how to work and the church will teach them how to rest and be refreshed. This is not possible because the two belong together inseparably. It is necessary to learn to work well in order that we may rest well. It is not possible just to work well and at the same time neglect the day earmarked for rest and refreshment. Life is all of a piece. Still, it is necessary to say some-

52

thing first about the believer's work and then about the believer's rest. First then, a few biblical truths about the Christian's work, and then a few thoughts about his rest.

The biblical position beyond a doubt favors work. It is against idleness, against the wasting of time, against living off somebody else's sweat, against wastefulness. Many believe that it was the socialists who coined the phrase, "If anyone will not work, let him not eat." But these words come from the Bible. They can be found in 2 Thessalonians 3:10, R.S.V. The Bible is *for* work. But the Bible is a critical book. Along with its yes, it has some negative things to say, and these too we have to take into account. Man is tempted by work, as well as by idleness. In theological language we would say that work has its own demonic dimension. Just as money, power, the body, have their demonic dimension, even so does work. Work too can swallow up a man, so that he is unable to rest. Against this temptation, the Bible says, "Six days you shall labor, and do all your work; but the seventh day . . . you shall not do any work." The Bible takes a stand in favor equally of work and of rightful rest.

Another critical perspective which the Bible offers is the necessity of evaluating work and the fruits of work from the standpoint of faith. When the Bible speaks of work, it points back toward the creation and at the same time, forward toward the new creation, toward our redemption. With respect to work, this means, "Man, you did not create the world. You only appeared in the world which God had created. Don't forget that you are a creature, that you are God's partner at work. God goes before you, his work precedes yours." Thus the Bible points back toward the creation. It points forward toward the new creation by saying, "Man, you are not redeeming the world. God has redeemed the world. God is bringing forth a new heaven and a new earth. You have the opportunity to participate in God's redemptive work."

These are critical thoughts, which are not particularly welcome these days. But if we would be faithful to the Bible, we must take them into account. We must keep in mind that the Bible would have us labor for six days and stop on the seventh, sanctifying that day to God. Man's dignity rests upon his ability to work as well as his ability to lay down his work and rest. Where work and rest are not in harmony, there is no human dignity. Let us read a few verses from Psalm 127. This Psalm offers unmistakable evidence of the Bible's thought regarding work and God.

> Unless the LORD builds the house,
>    those who build it labor in vain.
> Unless the LORD watches over the city,
>    the watchman stays awake in vain.
> It is in vain that you rise up early
>    and go late to rest,
> eating the bread of anxious toil;
>    for he gives to his beloved sleep (R.S.V.).

I hope I don't have to explain that this Psalm does not express opposition to work. The Word of God here is concerned with what may be missing from our work—in biblical language, God's blessing —and that if this blessing from above, this divine approval, is missing, we may break our backs working, and still our work will not bear fruit. Thus the Bible is concerned not only with work, but with the fact that work takes place either within the love of God or under his judgment.

And it is vain to work against the judgment of God. *We need God's blessing upon our work*, and it is in this connection that we note the words of the fourth commandment, "therefore the LORD blessed the sabbath day and hallowed it." In other words, the presence of God's blessing during the first six days depends also upon what happens on the seventh. God blesses the man who knows how to rest in him, who turns to him thoughtfully, in search of his truths. The work of this man will be productive and fruitful.

Above the entrance to the College of Debrecen there is the inscription ORA ET LABORA—"pray and work." It is in the union of these two that man is blessed. Therefore we must learn how to rest properly on the seventh day so that our labor during the next six may also be blessed. And here let me repeat what I said at the beginning of our study of the Ten Commandments, that it is not God who needs them, we do. It is not necessary for God that the bells be rung on Sunday and that everyone turn to him, each in his own way, in prayer. The Ten Commandments are not designed to further God's interests, lest he become a kind of orphan. On the contrary, God gave us the Ten Commandments to further our interests. He gave them so that we might become human. And part of our becoming human is to work and then stop and think and rest. And then of course we work again, and again we think and stand before God, and once more we return to the world. Man does not live by bread alone, but by every word that proceeds from the mouth of God. We live by bread and we live by the Word of God. And he who does well by both his daily bread and the bread of life has achieved a fully human life.

Thus, now that I'm about to comment upon the sanctification of the seventh day, I will again look at the problem not from God's point of view, in terms of what we must give to him on the seventh day, but in terms of our human needs. What happens to the man who duly sanctifies the seventh day? I have a simple formula that I have shared with you before and will now repeat in condensed form: We fill up with heavenly things.

I would like you to take this simple image home with you: We fill up with heavenly things; that is, we're being filled up not from any human gas station but from a heavenly supply. We get a tankful of spiritual energy—and we need it. We can only live like human beings for six days if on the seventh we replenish our supply of heavenly matter. Of course this is something we need during the six days as well, but God has appointed a special day in which we may rest from our work and replenish our store of heavenly things so that we may then return to our workaday life with new strength. What is the sanctification of the seventh day? It is to be refilled with spiritual energy.

Now the Pharisees wanted to look upon the Sabbath at all costs from the standpoint of "God's glory." So they said, "On the Sabbath it is not permitted to put any beast of burden to work nor to pull a man or beast out of a ditch, because God's glory is more important than the interests of either man or beast." But Jesus said, "Yes it is permissible to do good on the Sabbath, because the Sabbath was made for man rather than man for the Sabbath." The Sabbath was given so that we might live humanly. It is a gift, not a rigid law. God gave us the Sabbath that we might not lose our human dignity but lead a rich, common, harmonious life. And the key to this life is to be filled anew one day out of seven with spiritual energy, with heavenly things.

It is interesting to realize how eloquently the human body "preaches" to the same effect. Biologists tell us that during the day we expend energy, which then we replenish at night, but that every day we expend more energy than we are able to regain during the night. Therefore from time to time it is in the interests of our bodies to lay down our work and replenish our store of energy. Physicians today regard the nervous system with its millions of little nerve cells as an electrical system, with each cell as a little battery filled with nervous energy. During the day while we work, worry, and get tired, the battery's store is depleted, there is loss of energy. At night the battery receives a recharge, but not enough of a recharge. Therefore it is necessary, even from the standpoint of natural science, to set aside the seventh day so that these millions of little cells, these wonderful little batteries, may be properly recharged, and so that during the next week the process of daily spending more than we're able to regain may begin anew. Thus I'd like to say that the human body is preaching to us. Study the nervous system; the law of the seventh day is written into it. It is not God who gets hurt when you do not observe the seventh day. It is you who will experience nervous exhaustion and high blood pressure, and eventually it is you who will be disabled from working altogether. God's holy law stands fast and is written into every one of our nerve cells. So think of each nerve cell as a little battery from which flows the energy you need to do your work, but which from time to time must be recharged. This is the biological meaning of the sanctification of the seventh day.

But the spiritual meaning can be formulated in the same way. During any service of worship our hearts fill up with good intentions, with faith, love, forgiveness, and we resolve that we will live in obedience to the Word of God. But don't you feel how during the week this store of spiritual things diminishes? The level of our faith goes down, so that we must return to God in order to be filled up once more. The sanctification of the Sabbath is not a religious duty, but a rule for living, a rule which can be spiritually authenticated as well as biologically accounted for. The human organism is so oriented that every so often it is necessary for us to be refilled, for always we expend more than we take in.

At this point I would like to talk about the commandment in quite practical terms. I will lay aside theology, even though many interesting things might be said about how the Jews are observing Saturday whereas we observe Sunday, the day of the resurrection. But I prefer to continue at this time in a concrete way to comment on what it means to fill up with heavenly things, how it is done and what it involves. This filling-up process has both a negative and a positive side. The negative side we may call loosening up, getting rid of our cramped-up state. Filling up, then, is the positive side; the observance of the seventh day consists on the one hand in relaxing our tension and on the other hand in storing up new powers in order to gain momentum for the work of the next six days.

What do I mean by loosening up, by freeing one's self from cramped-up conditions? I'll define what I mean by giving three illustrations. In the first place we must free ourselves from the bondage of work. There are people who can't stop, who are forever being driven. This is like a cramp which we must learn to relax. The world will still be there, even though I take Sunday off.

In the second place we must free ourselves from our obsession with money. Often the reason behind the way I drive myself is that I believe I must absolutely have that money. But a Christian man has to consider: "Do I really have to run with the crowd just to get that and that and that?" If we stop to think, we realize that they are struggling people who live in such misery that they are literally fighting for every bite of food. Let us honor them and let us be sure that any society which is so ordered that it does not permit its members to earn a living wage during six days is under judgment. It is not always those who work on the seventh day who are really at fault. Too many people are so spellbound by money that they are saying, "Sunday is a good day to make money; the pay is better, and I need the money." But a part of sanctifying that day is extricating ourselves from this spell.

In the third place we must relax the grip which our worries have upon us. I must realize that everything does not turn around me or depend on me and that no irreparable harm will come to the world if I take Sunday off.

In order to keep the seventh day holy, it is necessary therefore that we stop being slaves to our work, to money, and to our worries. But this is only the negative part of the commandment—the relaxing of our cramped state. Then we must fill up with heavenly things. And here again I will submit three thoughts. According to my experience the sanctification of the Lord's Day consists of three things: thought, prayer, and play. This third one may surprise you but I believe that you will agree with me.

In the first place to be filled up on Sunday, I must first of all think about my own affairs. I must give an account of the week that is past, of the direction of my life. I must confront myself, give an account of myself.

In the second place there is prayer. This means that in this process of accounting I do not remain within my own little circle, but rather seek God's light. I ask forgiveness for the sins of the week that is past, with which I have grieved God and hurt my fellowmen. I beg for vision, that I may properly understand my life. I ask for the power of the Holy Spirit, that my life may be filled with new zest, new joy, new will. Thus, on the one hand I examine myself, and on the other hand I stand before God and ask him for strength.

In the third place there is play. Unfortunately this concept is usually limited to card-playing, drinking, and carousing. But I say that a Christian must learn to relax and to fill up in this way so that when he is with people, he is able to enjoy their company freely, serenely, so that both his soul and theirs are filled with fresh joys. Those who attempt to sanctify Sunday by playing cards or doing other such things are putting a good thing to bad use. The good thing is that they are seeking joy, that they are seeking to be filled. But they pursue this good goal by artificial means.

Christians have to learn to be together joyfully, light-heartedly, for in this experience there is something truly supernatural. It grieves me to realize how many Christians think that the sanctification of the Lord's Day is exclusively a matter of praying. It is my belief that all three things are needed: the encounter with one's self, the search for God in prayer, and some free happy fellowship with others whose purpose is not to do anything specific, let alone to make money, but just to enjoy one another's company freely and happily. This is my understanding of what it means to hallow the seventh day. We free ourselves of the bondage in which work, money, and worry have held us and, through meditation, prayer, and serene playful togetherness, we are replenished with new strength.

One further thought, in closing: In the fourth chapter of the Letter to the Hebrews we read about the day of rest. We read: "So then, there remains a sabbath rest for the people of God; for whoever enters God's rest also ceases from his labors as God did from his. Let us therefore strive to enter that rest . . ." (R.S.V.). The people of God have a Sabbath that is neither the Jewish Sabbath nor the Christian Sunday. The meaning of this verse is that our whole way of life is supposed to be rest, God's rest. As long as we did not know our Heavenly Father through Jesus Christ we were nervous, we were possessed of an ancient restlessness and fear, and thus we were being driven on weekdays and Sundays alike. But when we were redeemed, so the Letter tells us, we entered into God's rest, we attained rest: "God is my Father, I need not fear. My life does not depend on my own two hands; it is not my work that is redeeming the world. Redeemed men enter into God's rest. God is my Father; I am living in his house. The order decreed by my heavenly Father stands fast: 'Six days you shall labor . . . but the seventh day you shall not do any work.' I have entered into God's rest."

Whenever Seventh-Day Adventists ask me why we do not observe Saturday but Sunday, I always tell them that the question is really in error because we are not observing either Saturday or Sunday: *our whole life is rest in God.* The grip of fear has been relaxed in our life. We are no longer in the race. Our whole life is in a sense a holiday, a "holy day." The work we perform during six days is not foreign; it too is worship. I live in my father's house and, when I work, I work with my eyes upon the Father, and in obedience to him. And my whole life is filled with that sense of rest that comes from knowing I'm in God's hands. And he whose whole life "rests" in God knows how to observe the seventh day wisely.

Observance of the seventh day does not take place at the level of the Old Covenant. The fulfillment of the commandment becomes possible through Jesus Christ. It is in him that my life has found rest. I'm a sinful man of unclean heart, worthy of judgment, but I'm God's child; God loves me; God has taken my life in hand and he cleanses me. I live in God's rest. In this rest do I labor and in this rest, too, my strength is renewed on the seventh day.

May God so bless you that above all you may be able to live your life in his rest. Then you will see how good it is to come forth from this rest to do your work for six days, and again how good it is to spend the seventh day in the happiness of replenishment. How very good indeed it is to be filled again and again with God's peace and God's strength!

# V

# TO HONOR—IN FREEDOM

Exodus 20:12

"Honor your father and your mother, that your days may be long in the land which the LORD your God gives you" (R.S.V.).

According to traditional religious thinking, in this commandment God takes the part of the parents; he wants to secure their authority against rebellious children. That is how we learned it in our childhood and that is the common assumption. But I would like you to bid a final farewell to this interpretation, so that you might recognize and accept the true content and message of the commandment.

First of all we have to answer the question, "Who is the 'you' whom God is addressing in the Ten Commandments?" For God always addresses somebody. Who is the "you" to whom God speaks in all ten of the commandments? God did not address these words to the air; he did not give them to mankind in general. No, the Ten Commandments were given to the Covenant people within the solemnity of the making of the Covenant. By the intermediary of Moses, God made a Covenant with the people of Israel at Mount Sinai and he gave them the Ten Commandments as a part of this Covenant. But who are these Covenant partners of God whom he addresses as "you"?

We may divide the complex unity of the Jewish people who

61

were encamped at the foot of Mount Sinai into three groups. We might place in the middle those who were taking an active part in the people's life. These were the men who would fight when it was necessary to fight, who would work when there was work to do, who would make and break camp. They were the active, working part of the people. Then there was a group of little ones who were not working yet. These were the children, the babies, and there was a group of old people who were no longer working. The Jewish camp could be divided into these three groups.

Now then, when God speaks to the people, to which group among the three is he likely to speak? Obviously to the active group. God makes his Covenant with the workers, the fighters, the functioning part of the nation. Of course, the Covenant will have consequences for both the children and the old people, but as a Covenant, it is concerned with the people in their prime.

Last Sunday we were talking about the fourth commandment, ". . . in it you shall not do any work, you, or your son, or your daughter, your manservant, or your maidservant." God was addressing himself to the men who had sons and daughters. To be sure, children have a part to play in this connection. This is why we read from Deuteronomy, "When your son asks you in time to come, 'What is the meaning of the testimonies and the statutes and the ordinances which the LORD our God has commanded you?' then you shall say to your son . . ." (R.S.V.). God addresses himself, in the first place, to the people in their prime: "But if your son asks you what this is all about, it is your responsibility to explain to him how God has made a covenant with you"; and, ". . . you shall teach them diligently to your children, and shall talk of them when you sit in your house, and when you walk by the way, and when you lie down, and when you rise" (R.S.V.). God is telling us that we should teach the commandments to our children, but when he first gave them to his people he was addressing himself to the adults among them. This simple fact is quite obvious from the text, but it has enormous consequences. For if this be so, the commandment applies first of all not to children, but to fathers and mothers, indeed to grandfathers and grandmothers. Therefore let us say a resolute goodbye to that interpretation of the commandment according to which God is telling the kids "where to get off"! This is not the case at all. God is here speaking to fathers and mothers: "Honor your father and your mother." He is not telling children that they should honor adults. Rather he is telling *adults* that they should honor their *elders*.

This had to be clarified in order that we might understand the commandment in its original biblical context. God is saying, "You, my Covenant people, who have children of your own, I'm telling you to honor your fathers and mothers." Of course it is possible to extend the meaning of the commandment to children, but let us not forget that the commandment applies first of all to adults whose fathers and mothers are alive.

In order to enter completely into the meaning of this commandment and to grasp the divine thought which it harbors, it is necessary to remind ourselves of another, similarly important truth that God reveals in the very first pages of the Bible where we read about marriage. There we find the statement, "Therefore a man leaves his father and his mother and cleaves to his wife . . ." (R.S.V.). He *leaves* his father and his mother and he *honors* his father and his mother. Let us connect these two insights. This is not an arbitrary decision on my part; usually we forget that they belong together. God's thought is that when a man and a woman found a new family, they leave their parents on the one hand, but on the other hand they look back upon them and honor them. God, then, intends parents to leave their parents *and* to honor them. And the whole truth of the commandment is summed up in this dialectic.

Let us think about it. It is not good if someone is unable to leave his father and mother, if he honors them till their dying day so much that, in the language of psychology, he cannot cut the cord. And there are people like that. They honor their parents so much that they cannot leave them. That is just as bad as the opposite, when someone leaves his father and mother in such a way that he no longer honors them. Either extreme can cause an endless amount of family problems and miseries. It is bad when a man is unable to leave his father and mother, when he honors them in that, like a baby, he remains ever in the presence of their authority. But it is equally bad when someone leaves his father and mother in a harsh and brutal rebellion, no longer honoring them. But extremes are temptingly easy, while it is hard to observe God's order. It is easy to kick over all family loyalty and to cease honoring one's parents. And it is easy to remain so closely tied to father and mother that they are in effect living our lives for us. But it is difficult to leave father and mother in such a way that we continue to honor them. In other words, God's order, according to the witness of this commandment, is that every new family is supposed to shape its own life in its own freedom and humanity, and, within this new life, honor those who have been left behind. This is God's thought on the matter.

In order to shed further light upon this truth, let me refer to a different system of thought. For there are alternatives. There are other religions, with other judgments upon the subject. Let us see if we can illuminate the truth of this commandment by contrasting it with insights drawn from a different faith. I'm referring to the religion of China, Confucianism, which makes a great deal of the honor which must be shown to parents. Historians of religion have proved beyond a doubt that the very first thesis of ancient Chinese ethics was that parents were always right. The parents had all the rights, and woe to the child who would rebel, who would not obey his parents. I'm going to tell you a story which illustrates this entire mind set.

A Chinese father was very poor. He was living with his father and his children in the utmost misery and hunger. His problem was whether to give the little food he had to his father or to his children. And, according to the story, the Chinese father decided to bury his children alive in order to feed his father. But while he was digging their graves, his spade struck an object which turned out to be a box full of treasures. For the gods accepted the sacrifice and blessed him who fulfilled the law. The father had no responsibility toward his children, only toward his parents. This is basic in Confucian ethics.

And the implications are that parents can do whatever they please with their children. They can sell them, they can kill them, without being called to law for it. But woe to the child who raises a hand against his parents! I read somewhere that in 1882 the following incident occurred. A Chinese young man went home drunk. His mother scolded him for being drunk, whereupon the young man struck her. The mother began to cry for help, the men assembled, bound the boy, and buried him alive. And all the people watched the show as a dramatic illustration of the existing order. The mother had a right to bury alive the child who had raised a hand against her. It was a completely authoritarian society. All the rights belonged to the parents, and the children owed them an unconditional, total obedience.

In contrast to this system, let us look again at the biblical word which says, "Honor your father and your mother," and, ". . . a man shall leave his father and mother and be joined to his wife" (R.S.V.). How is a home founded within the framework of a patriarchal society, and how is a home founded according to biblical insights? In a patriarchal system the family is a large circle. The founding of a new home means that somewhere *within* this large circle an individual gets married, and, as a result, someone new enters the circle. But it is father and mother who continue to rule. The circle has not been broken, it has only been enlarged. This is the patriarchal system of Confucianism. In contrast, the biblical model is this: There is the family circle, with the members within the circle. A marriage is concluded. Someone steps *outside* the circle and causes a new circle to be formed outside the old circle; and it is this new circle which looks back with reverence upon the old. There is an enormous difference between these two worlds of thought. And I'm telling you that it is God's thought that makes the difference.

If we look more closely at the Jewish people, we see that they too have been influenced by the patriarchal mode of thought. But God imparted to them his thought—and his thought was not patriarchal, but dialectic. A member steps outside the family circle, founds a new family, and the members of this family circle are supposed to honor their parents. Perhaps this offends the traditional thinking of some of you. If this be so, I respect your perplexity, but I'm fully convinced that this is the message of the commandment: that leaving behind my father and my mother I go on to found a new family, and that it is from this place that I look back, with reverence, upon the family circle where I grew up.

Anyone who follows me this far will have no trouble deriving all the necessary applications from the principle. We do not have time to make applications now. My chief concern is that we understand the principle. We leave our fathers and mothers, found our own homes, and it is this new family which is bidden by God, "Honor your father and your mother." All that remains for us to do is to clarify the meaning of the word "honor."

What is involved in honoring our fathers and our mothers? Here again I shall first point to the extremes between which the true meaning of this word may be found: self-centered rebellion against parents and blind obedience to them. It is my conviction that "Honor your father and your mother" offers a perceptive dialectic between these extremes. It suggests both wise rebellion and wise obedience. On the one hand, I'm supposed to rebel—but with respect and love, even while I resolutely affirm that I have outgrown this circle and am now responsible for a family of my own, that I interpret my life in a different way. On the other hand, I'm supposed to obey wisely: "I yield to you not because you are my father or mother and have authority over me, but because I too have arrived at the insights which you have achieved; and thus I obey the things which you yourself obey."

Let us remember what the tone used to be in our homes: "Shut up, kid; I'm your father, I'm giving the orders! What right have you to talk back to me?" In other words, there was a complete dictatorship by the parents. Today, on the other hand, we have a complete dictatorship by the children. "By what right are you meddling with my life?" a child asks. And when a girl comes home at daybreak, she says about her mother, "Boy, was the old lady mad!" What do we have today? We have an absolute dictatorship by the children. But I believe that we realize how bad both extremes are. The time is past when parents lorded it over their children. And let us not imagine that that was a Christian world and the one we live in today is pagan! That world was just as pagan as ours is. What God is saying in this commandment means that God is not partial. He wants to teach both parents and children to live the good life. God says, "Honor your father and your mother," and that means that you have a right to shape your own life, that this, indeed, is your task as a man. But at the same time you are supposed to remember with respect those who in their day shaped their own life and made sacrifices for you because they wanted to transmit a good inheritance to you. You have every right to examine the value of the thoughts, the truths, which they bequeath to you, but you must do it with respect.

And here we face the problem of authority. There is a great deal of complaining today that children no longer respect the authority of their parents. But let us see whether parents have any authority just because they are parents. Is a mother supposed to have authority just because she has given birth to a child? Certainly not. If parents have no higher authority to which they themselves bow down, they should not expect their children to bow down before them. To be a parent does not, in itself, entitle one to authority. These days a thirteen-year-old child will ask his parents: "Why did you bring me into the world? Did I want to be born? Just because you brought me into the world doesn't mean that you can claim any authority over me."

This is God's order: If parents bow to a higher authority and their children see it, then the parents will have authority over their children. Under wholesome conditions—and I regard Christian conditions as wholesome conditions—parents can say: "Children, we are seeking the truth. We are trying to lead the good life, and here are some of the conclusions at which we have arrived: It is a good thing to love God; it is a good thing not to do anyone any harm; it is a good thing to forgive. We are seeking the truth and we have discovered some. We cannot follow all the way, but we would like to be obedient to the truth and to share our experiences with you so that you might do likewise."

If parents speak in this manner, they will have authority. Or, more correctly, it will be not the parents but the truth the parents seek that will have authority. Authority does not depend upon the status of parents, but upon God. If God has no authority for the parents, then let them be prepared not to have any authority for their children. If a child sees that his parents are seeking the truth but are unable to obey it all the way, and they honestly tell him, "I hope you will do better," the child will respect them. But if a parent says to his child, "You miserable scoundrel, you're always lying! I never lied!" the parent should not be surprised if he has no authority. After all, he lied to his child and the child saw through the lie. We can claim no authority over our children just on the basis that we conceived and bore them. Authority must be earned; it cannot simply be demanded. If I strive for truth in my life and am duly penitent—"I'm not making it, my child, but I do hope you will do better"—then there is hope that God may secretly kindle a deep respect in my children for me. In other words, this commandment does not suggest that God is taking sides, the side of parents against children. Rather the commandment talks about what it means to become human. It is another divine help for our struggle in that direction.

To sum up once more: Whoever has been unable to separate himself from his parents and start to live his own life has not really become human. On the other hand, whoever has kicked over everything, turning his back upon his parents in a grand show of radicalism, has not really become human either. God's order calls for connection, relationship, continuity. Our lives are being built upon the labors and failures, the sins and forgiveness of sins, of prior generations. Whoever would become human will contemplate with respect the strivings, the weariness, the failures, the mistakes, the quest, of former generations while he builds his own life. If I cannot tear myself away from the previous generation, I have not become a complete man; and if I radically repudiate everything that has gone before me, I'm not completely human either. And the latter is quite fashionable now at times. Radical individualism is like fine sand, which indeed is not attached to anything and so is blown hither and yon by the slightest breeze. Such a radical individual is not really human.

"Honor your father and your mother" means that you are permitted to build a better world than your father and mother built, that you are free to lead a nobler, purer life than they lived. But if you really aspire to such a higher life, you will learn to appreciate how your father and mother struggled while they were trying to shape their lives. Yes, and you are free to bring up your children better than your father and mother brought you up. But in your struggle to bring up your children and in the failures which will inevitably attend this struggle, you will learn to appreciate the struggle which your father and mother had in trying to bring you up. This is the continuity we are talking about, that we seek that which is better but, while we fail to attain it, we develop a greater appreciation for those who went before us. This too is God's thought on the matter.

Only that person will despise his forebears who has not created anything better, and who is not even attempting to create anything better. But if you say, "I would like to bring up my children better than my father and mother brought me up, but I wonder whether I will succeed" or if you honestly face your failures and admit that you are not doing very well, *then* you will begin deeply to appreciate and love your father and your mother. Thus the process consists of a gradual liberation from the thinking and the methods of our parents and, at the same time, of an ever-deepening respect for their strivings. This dialectic unity is the divine meaning of the commandment.

# VI
## YOU SHALL NOT KILL!

Exodus 20:13

"You shall not kill" (R.S.V.).

Week after week the conviction grows in me that as soon as this series of sermons is over, I will have to start another series under the title "What has been omitted from the series on the Ten Commandments"! Every Sunday I have the feeling that I would like to say so much more than I was able to. This is how it will be again today. And, God willing, I will indeed offer another series later under the heading "What has been omitted."

By way of introduction let me point out to you a few themes about which one absolutely must speak in connection with the commandment "You shall not kill," so that you may realize how many problems are hidden behind these few words. The problem of war belongs to this commandment, together with its horrible modern version—nuclear war. We shall not ask ourselves whether or not war can be justified. For today it is beyond a doubt that war *cannot* be justified from the entire text of Scripture, nuclear war least of all. The problem is rather what the attitude of the Christian community should be toward a state which is preparing for nuclear warfare. It would seem that this commandment orders us to resist actively a state that prepares to commit mass murder by this means.

But the problem of capital punishment also relates to this commandment. To what extent does the state have a right to exact such punishment?

The problem of suicide also appears. How should we think of those who choose to throw away their lives? And another painful, miserable Hungarian problem—the problem of abortion—also comes to mind in this connection. And the same may be said of the problem of contraception.

I might add a few more questions. For example, Is it permissible to kill a tyrant? Did Brutus do the right thing when he killed Julius Caesar? In the context of modern technology is it possible for a man to resort to arms in order to deliver a community from a tyrant?

Again, the question of euthanasia arises. Is it permissible to hasten death by medical means? And this of course has a coarser version as well: May the state pass a law to get rid of harmful people by rendering them sterile?

You see how many problems are conjured up by these few words, "You shall not kill"!

It is obvious that all these problems cannot be dealt with within a single sermon. However, they are all actually branches, ramifications, and I would like to point to the root from which they spring. Once you understand the root, you will be able to understand the meaning of the ramifications. Therefore we shall limit ourselves to the root. That is what I would like to reveal in the light of Scripture, in the light of the gospel.

It is my conviction that the words of our Lord Jesus Christ will lead us to the root. In the Gospel of Matthew, chapter 5, we read,

> You have heard that it was said to the men of old, "You shall not kill; and whoever kills shall be liable to judgment." But I say to you that every one who is angry with his brother shall be liable to judgment; whoever insults his brother shall be liable to the council, and whoever says, "You fool!" shall be liable to the hell of fire. So if you are offering your gift at the altar, and there remember that your brother has something against you, leave your gift there before the altar and go; first be reconciled to your brother, and then come and offer your gift (R.S.V.).

The most striking thing in this biblical passage usually escapes us: that when Jesus talks about anger—from which murder comes—and when he talks about people who are angry with each other, he is not talking about mankind in general, but about *brothers*. If you are angry with your brother, your own flesh and blood, you are liable to judgment. As if Jesus thought that brothers enjoy hating each other! As if Jesus had had experiences that had taught him that those who dwell under the same roof are likely to have severe tensions between them. For he is saying in effect that those who live under the same roof—brothers, or married people—indulge in hate, which is the root of murder.

Let us conjure up a very ordinary everyday scene. Husband and wife are quarreling bitterly, venomously, loudly. The doorbell rings and an unexpected guest arrives. What happens? Quickly they smooth out their distorted features and put on the act of a loving couple living a life of peace and love. Company comes and temporarily there is peace. But then company leaves and the tension resumes. What this means is that the stranger somehow serves as insulating material. He takes his place between the poles which stand in awesome tension one with the other, and while he is there there is no explosion. If a couple cannot restrain themselves even before strangers, they're indeed in a very sad way. What is the meaning of this phenomenon? This is what Jesus has in mind. This is where murder begins, this is the *root* of the matter. And the question is not very hard to answer.

What this all means is that I want to live and that your presence is a disturbing element in my life. You mean competition for me. Because of you, I cannot really live. The result is friction, collision. A little child experiences it in this way: "If I did not have a brother, I would get more chocolate. This way I have to share with him." Brother means competition. When the firstborn falls from his pedestal as "only child," because now there is another, he has fits of jealousy and literally wants to kill his little brother. Now then, what little children experience unchecked, without putting on any act, is what causes tensions in human society. This image is portrayed for us with fearful realism in the Old Testament in the story of Cain and Abel. Cain felt that even God loved his brother more than he loved him, and it was unbearable for him that because of his brother he was not getting enough of life. His brother was breathing his air, eating his bread, robbing him of God's blessing. Therefore his brother had to die!

Jesus is right, therefore, when he tells us that anger exists first of all among brothers, among members of the same family, and that strangers have, if anything, a calming effect. Brothers hate each other because they are convinced—with a conviction which may not be uttered—that because of the other, there is less for one's self; and should the other die, one would have more. This is the archetypal image of murder: "If he disappears, I alone will be here to enjoy the inheritance." This is the root of our subject. Fallen, sinful, benighted man thinks, "He must die so that I may enjoy a more complete life. His death will solve my problem." This has been glossed over by culture; it has been forced down into the depths of the subconscious. But there it survives and continues to work. "His death will solve my problem."

Now then, it is to this impulse of fallen man that the word of God, "You shall not kill," is addressed. What God is saying here may be put into words in Old Testament style in this way: "Men, make no mistake! Do not believe that his death will bring you life, progress, happiness!"

But let me try to translate this message into the style, the negative form, of the New Testament. The Old Testament says, "It is not true that his death will solve your problems. It is not true that if you sacrifice him upon the altar of your selfishness you will be happy. It is not true that you must kill him in order that you might truly live." But along comes the New Testament and complements the ancient truths in a wondrous, positive manner. Through the words, the story, the cross, the resurrection of Jesus Christ, the New Testament tells us, on the contrary, *"Your own willingly incurred death is what will solve your problem.* If you can sacrifice yourself for him, you have found the solution."

These connections are truly wonderful. Stupid man thinks, "If I liquidate him, I'll be happy." The Old Testament says, "You're mistaken, man; that will not get you any further." But the New Testament sets forth the truths of Jesus: "The only solution is for you to sacrifice yourself for the sake of your brother. If someone can give his life for another, that solves the problem, that is life."

Let me sharpen up this dual truth even further. The Old Testament says, "If you think that by killing him you will solve your problem, you're in effect mobilizing *demonic forces* and they will be filling your life." But the New Testament says, "If you sacrifice yourself for his sake, *heavenly powers* will be set into motion and will bless you with resurrection and a wonderful new life; and they will also bless him whom you may now regard as your enemy."

Let me illustrate this truth by two examples, the first, from the smallest human circle—the family—and, specifically, the problem of abortion. The problem is that I do not want to be responsible for a child and that, if one should appear, I will kill it. Why? Because it means competition, because it endangers my "chocolate." I will kill it because I want to live, and I see the arrival of a child as a threat. He will shorten my life. Therefore let him die so that I may live. Of course, these things are seldom spoken so harshly, but here, at least, let us call a spade a spade. (Of course the situation may be entirely honorable when the question is whether the life of the child or of the mother should be saved by sacrificing the other life; at which point it becomes the responsibility of the physician to decide which life should be sacrificed.) Now, however, we are talking about the situation when the question is, "Baby or car? Shall we have a child or shall we have an automobile?" In this case, a child means competition, for he will make it impossible for the parents to get a car. So he must die that the parents may live. It is in this case that the Old Testament says, "You are wrong; your life will not be enriched in any way if you kill your offspring, but rather if you accept God's gift and assume responsibility for it." And the New Testament says, "You would awaken to a wonderful new life, if you could 'die' for the sake of the child."

Or, for a different interpretation: If you kill a child in your own self-interest, you are releasing demonic powers which sooner or later will destroy you, together with your family, your wealth, your car. But if you willingly sacrifice yourself for the child, heavenly powers will come to your aid. God's blessing, love, joy, will be yours. This is the biblical message.

Now let us take an illustration from the largest human circle; let us look briefly at the problem of war. There again the problem is competition which is supposed to threaten my life. The competition must be destroyed so that I may lead a rich life. This is where we have been engaging in the dreadful practice of exterminating the competition. It matters little under the banner of which ideology this is taking place. Let us be objective enough to admit that this is what is happening. It is because of my competitor that I cannot develop fully. Therefore he must be subdued, he must be liquidated, for then I shall be great and happy. This has been the horrible basic thrust of all human history. This is the insane thinking which is carrying human history toward ultimate catastrophe— that if I kill him, I will be better off.

Let us think of the dreadful international tension, the nuclear weapons race, the failure to find peace, in the midst of which we live. The actual fighting is far from us, but don't you feel the demonic powers which are filling the whole earth? Don't you feel Satan's own fire even here? Yes, we are feeling the fires of hell in our own lives. And it is a frightening feeling. For war requires hate. Soldiers must be schooled in hate in order that they may fight with passion. Therefore I must repeat the same truth: Nothing would be solved if the United States were to succeed in driving all Communists out of Vietnam. Nothing would be solved. But even now awful demonic powers have been let loose and they're encircling the entire world. Everyone must hate, this way or that way. It is not possible to live with an affirmation of life. It is necessary to live with a commitment against life. Thus what is true within the family circle is equally true in the world of nations—murder and death solve nothing. And this is true in the individualistic selfishness of abortion just as much as in the collective madness of war. God's message is, "You shall not kill." Do not ever believe that another's death will solve your problems.

I might briefly mention that the commandment includes not only, "You shall not kill another," but also, "You shall not kill yourself." For man is so stupid that he does even this. What does it mean, that you shall not kill yourself? I'm thinking not only of suicide when a man puts a quick end to himself, but of suicide when a man spends a lifetime killing himself, continuous suicide. Let me give an example from the life of the body. If someone ties off the circulation anywhere in his body, he'll soon be in trouble. If he ties off the very last digit of his little finger, he's taking it out of the circulation of the blood, and soon that small part will die, and from there death will spread through his entire system. You can kill yourself by tying off the tip of your little finger.

This can be interpreted as a parable and applied to all of life. It is God's intention that we should have life and that we should have it abundantly. God would have us live a rich, throbbing life. We dare not tie off any part of our spiritual life because whatever we shut out of our life, whatever we suppress in our life against God's will, will carry death into our entire life. I read a report by a psychiatrist. He was telling a surprising story about a very rich merchant—in the West—who appeared in his office with complaints about irregular heartbeat, stomach pains, and sleeplessness. He was asking for help. The psychiatrist began to question him, to make him tell the story of his life, and this is what came to light.

As a child, this rich man had liked to paint. But then he went into business, and business allowed no time for such a "hobby." His life was entirely taken up with business, but it appeared that he had "tied off" something. He had tied off a part of his true self. And from there death spread to his whole life. The psychiatrist figured it out. It was not just a matter of painting; painting in this case represented a whole way of life, a whole style of life. This man had been a seeker for beauty, he had spent time contemplating beauty, he had made time to try to understand the harmony of the universal order. While painting, this was the attitude toward life he was expressing. But he tied off this part of his life, he allowed the life of business to choke off this part, and soon another outlook came to dominate him, according to which it was necessary to overcome the competition, to watch out lest the enemy take away his wealth. Then came anxiety, the restless drive of the rat race, which was taking him straight toward death.

An instructive little story. God had given a destiny to this man. He gave him joy in painting, but the man—stupidly, for material interests—tied off his gift. And from there death spread through his entire life. How many men tie off in their soul this desire for God just because nowadays it is not profitable. They believe it is an unimportant part of life and can be bypassed with impunity. But whoever ties off the spiritual blood circulation is actually committing suicide in the worst possible sense of the word. For it is himself he puts to slow torture and death. Thus when we are told, "You shall not kill," this includes not only killing others but also killing ourselves!

In conclusion: Our basic concept is that the Ten Commandments talk not so much about God as they do about man. In the context of the question "How do we become human?" this commandment says to us, "Man, understand; you will not be truly human if you exterminate your competitor. For the secret of life is cooperation; it is to discover the brother in him whom you perceive as your enemy. You should find God's gift in him, make sacrifices for him, live for him. Thus will you become human." The Old Testament puts it negatively: "You shall not kill! Do not kill him, because that solves nothing." Christ carries the thought further: "Learn to live for him. When for his sake you submerge yourself in a willing death, divine powers appear and give you new life. And this new life is truly human life, the life for which God created you!"

# VII

# YOU SHALL NOT COMMIT ADULTERY!

Exodus 20:14

"You shall not commit adultery" (R.S.V.).

The Ten Commandments are helps—divine helps for us so that we may become truly human. God does not intend primarily to chastise us nor to give us stark, rigid rules, but rather to offer us helps, to assist us in becoming human. My interpretation of the Ten Commandments is not that God cracked his whip ten times so that the human rabble might behave themselves. (Unfortunately many do interpret them this way.) My interpretation of the Ten Commandments, based upon my knowledge of God, is that God loves us. He wants us to become human. Therefore he addresses us, talks with us, and gives us revelation, guidance, direction, help. The giving of the Ten Commandments, these ten helps, is one expression of God's helpful love. In them God reveals the basic laws of human life, points out the fundamental problems, temptations, struggles, and in this way guides us toward a more complete humanity.

The Ten Commandments were engraved upon two tablets of stone. We usually teach our children that God wrote upon the first tablet those commandments that pertain to our communion with him, the first four, and on the second tablet six commandments that determine our relationship with our fellowmen. This division implies the truth that man can only become truly human if his relationship with God is set right so that his relationships with his fellowmen are ordered accordingly. To live in communion with God and in good relationship with one's fellowman: that is the meaning of the completely human life.

At the moment we are on the second tablet and at the third commandment it contains, "You shall not commit adultery." Let us consider this commandment.

Let me tell you in advance what my approach here will be. I do not wish to use it as an occasion for scolding sinners, even though this commandment has been known to offer an opportunity for certain preachers to scold the whole world. Many preachers seem to enjoy talking about wayward youth, crumbling morals, divorce statistics, the murder of children, in short, sin and damnation. I will not preach in this way. I hope rather to offer some help with the problems.

What is this commandment all about? What is my basic conviction with respect to sexuality? It is that the sexual instinct is a gift of God that he has given us truly as a gift for our enrichment and enjoyment. He has given it to us so that our life may be more human. He did not give it to us just so that we might have offspring —though this is one of the many misunderstandings which has had a great deal of currency. God gave it to us so that between husband and wife there might develop such an intimate human relationship as cannot be achieved, nor even imagined, otherwise. In short, the sexual instinct is a gift of God designed for the enrichment and enjoyment of a more and more human life.

The gifts of God have a way of spoiling in the hands of man. This gift, too, has spoiled. But now comes a truth which may be hard to accept. The case is not that God's gift has spoiled in the hands of the sons of this world and not, thank God, in the hands of the church. Here I must step out of the usual churchly way. My conception of the matter is different and I'm going to tell you what it is. I do not believe that all the sins are being committed outside these walls but not within them. I do not believe that in here we are leading a pure and holy life, whereas outside all are sinners. Or, to express it more modestly, that outside people are thinking corruptly, whereas in here we are thinking correctly. Extensive experience as a pastor has convinced me, alas, that the thinking is just as faulty within these walls as it is outside. To be sure, our thinking is defective in a different way, but it is a moral obligation for the church first to examine the defects in its own thinking and only then begin to scold the world—if there is any time left for such scolding. To put things more systematically: How is God's gift of sex spoiled in the world and how is it being corrupted at the hands of believing religious people? The difference is very easy to grasp. In the world the trouble is that the sexual instinct, sex, is being deified and thus made into something demonic. It becomes divinity, salvation, the only goal, the only joy in life. Sex is being deified in films, in literature, in practice—and as a result it becomes demonic.

Among us, however, there is fear of sex—and this is how we make sex into a demonic thing. For fear too can bring about this result. We tend to say that sex is something sinful, something awful; therefore, let us keep away from it, let us not even talk about it, let us be ashamed of it! And it is by this attitude that we are making it into a demonic thing. Thus sexuality becomes demonic in the world in one way, and in the church in a different way.

I have been able to do considerable preparation for this sermon. Let me share with you some of the things I have read. The most disturbing statement I found appeared in a book on ethics. The writer says, "If believers are afraid of this instinct, if they make this force into an enemy, the force in turn will make them into slaves." This is worth thinking about. During the Middle Ages, as a result of some faulty concept, the Church suddenly decreed priestly celibacy. It can be proved from history that witch burnings began at once! Thanks to depth psychology, it is easy to connect the two events. Celibacy meant that the sexual life of men was being artificially repressed—in the name of God. (It is true that some are called, individually, to continence, but to institutionalize continence, to force it indiscriminately upon everyone, means that an artificial barrier is being built against God-given instinctual forces.) But if such a barrier exists, the instinct leaps across the barrier so that artificially "sanctified" men will begin to see witches in all women, witches who tempt them and threaten their salvation. And fires are lit around stakes on which unfortunate women burn by the thousands.

As soon as the sexual instinct is decreed to be an enemy, as a result of faulty thinking and dogmatics, it indeed does become an enemy, a destructive force which enslaves men. No one has as much trouble with sex as the man who is always fighting it, for whom it has become a demonic thing. We dare not brag about how good we are, how much we know, how intelligent we are, how well we are doing: "Thank God that among us the good old-fashioned morality is still in force! Outside everything is crumbling, everything is coming to an end." No, I refuse to think in this way. For, unfortunately, the churches have to refer a great many neurotics to mental health clinics!

My starting point then is that it is necessary for the church to approach the subject in penitence, in love, in faithfulness to God and respect for the attainments of science, and in this spirit to explore the meaning of the commandment "You shall not commit adultery."

If we approach the problem in this frame of mind, we have to clarify first of all what the Old Testament meant. What did the seventh commandment mean in that world? But we must not stop there. We have Jesus Christ who gave us the true and final Word. Thus, starting from the teachings of the Old Testament, we must advance to what Jesus Christ is saying. Let us start on this path, and may God assist us in our exploration. All we can really hope to do is to take a few steps across the threshold of the subject. The subject is vast; it covers an enormous amount of ground, far too much to permit us to consider all the details.

First of all we are to realize that other translations are more faithful to the Hebrew original than the Hungarian translation, "Do not lead a life of promiscuity." The German translation of the commandment says, "You shall not commit adultery." Thus the subject is not man's love life in general, but marriage, the family. To define the import of the commandment precisely, we must acknowledge that it is designed not so much to prohibit the love life as to protect the family. According to superficial thinking, the two may be regarded as one. But they are not one, least of all in Hebrew thinking. Some of you may be offended if I tell you what the situation was in the Old Testament world and even in the lifetime of Jesus Christ.

Polygamy was the fundamental institution. There is no formal injunction against polygamy in the Bible. Hebrew law clearly specified the rights of various wives. And if we asked the scholars what the commandment "You shall not commit adultery" meant in the world of the Old Testament we would at once learn the perhaps painful truth about the historic meaning of the commandment, that a Jewish man was not supposed to become sexually involved with the wife (or fiancée—a highly favored status) of another Jewish man. The commandment did not say that he should not be sexually involved with a slave girl, or a prostitute, or a woman taken captive in war. There was no law against such liaisons, and men took ample advantage of them. In other words, it is a historic fact that the commandment does not attempt to regulate our love life but rather to protect the institution of marriage. More precisely still—going beyond individual cases, the commandment was designed to protect the purity, unity, and increase of the Jewish people as the chosen people of God. God was as much as saying, "Your love life is your own business, but the purity and increase of my chosen people is a religious matter. That is my business!" These are the facts of Old Testament life, and young Martin Luther expounded them clearly in his biblical studies. But if this is so, it is a disturbing thought. God places the family, the institution of marriage, and, to extend the concept to the whole human race, the continuation of humanity, under his protection; and he gives a commandment to this effect!

Now let us take a long leap from Old Testament times to modern Freudianism. How does Freud interpret man's love life? Freudian psychology affirms that the sexual instinct is a mighty source of energy. As the taut mainspring of a watch moves the entire watchwork, even so this energy keeps in motion man's entire life. Freud says that all of our life is being governed by this flow of energy. And this energy directs man primarily toward sexual experiences. But society raises prohibitions. It is not possible to give free reign to our sexuality. Thus a portion of this energy, of necessity, strays into our secondary, artificial channels, and in these channels the energy is transformed, sublimated. Thus it comes to the surface as cultural achievement, status seeking, lust for power, good deeds, morality, sympathy, or, according to Freud, even as religion. The driving force which lies at the depths of man's life can, by sublimation, appear as moral or religious achievement. It was Freud's conviction that to the extent that society raises barriers against the satisfaction of man's sexual need, man becomes sick. We would like to give free reign to our sexual instinct, but society does not permit this. Therefore, according to Freud, a part of this vital energy strays into strange, false channels—and the result is sickness. Thus there are nervous ills, spiritual tensions, neuroses.

To go one step further: Freud claims that the path to healing is plain. We must step across these barriers which society has erected and live out the instinct which is ours to live out. To this day, if a patient goes to a psychiatrist, whether Freudian or other, the answer to the problem is likely to be, "Get rid of your inhibitions. Live your life fully and you will be healthy." This is the diagnosis and the prescription. It says in effect, "That which has strayed from its intended path has to be led back into its proper sexual channel. Let us give free rein to the instinct and all will be well."

Now let us remember again the situation in Old Testament times. There, too, there was more sexual energy around than could be accommodated within the institution of marriage. And the Old Testament says, "I will not interfere with what you may be doing elsewhere, but do not plow into the marriage of another."

Since then, a few thousand years have elapsed, and what was then possible is no longer possible because the thinking of society, the official mores, do not permit it. To give just one example from the world of the Old Testament: In those days, there was a formal institution known as "marriage for a night." A Jewish man went on a trip. In the course of the journey he concluded marriage with a woman for one night. In the morning he made out an official divorce form for her—since a man could divorce a woman at any time. In this way the whole matter was blameless, morally, socially, and legally. Thus there were institutions in those days of which neither the sons of this world nor the believers know anything at all.

But the Bible addresses itself precisely to this Old Testament world: "You shall not commit adultery. You shall not break into the marriage of another. What you do with your love life is your own business."

But several thousand years have passed and what was permissible and possible in Old Testament times is no longer so. Therefore what shall we do? For Freud is right when he says that the social framework within which men must lead their love life is inadequate so far as expressing their entire sexual energy is concerned. There is always an energy surplus which causes a problem about which something has to be done. But what? That is a big question. This is where religion comes in. Religious thinking traditionally holds that the entire question is sinful. Even having sexual intercourse with your wife is almost a sin. Therefore control the impulse as best you can. He who has never touched a woman but only translates this energy into moral and religious action is the real saint. This is religious thinking. The whole matter is branded as sinful, and men are frightened away from it. But the energy remains within us and as a result there are explosions, there is illness. Freudianism —the recommendation that we give our sexual instinct free reign —is not a solution. Neither does a religion of rules—which suggests that we should control, indeed, kill, the instinct—offer a solution. One is as bad as the other, and that is the truth.

What does Jesus Christ say? As important as the Old Testament is for us, the Ten Commandments are not our ultimate authority. Our ultimate authority is Jesus Christ. And as a matter of fact, he had a great deal to say. But we have to admit honestly that much of what he said got lost. In fact, it got lost at the hands of the disciples. The teachings of Jesus were so new, so startling—they so consistently refused to fit into the moral categories with which the apostles had grown up—that after Jesus' ascension they brought back into use many thoughts for which he would not assume responsibility and blanketed with silence many others that he had proclaimed. Serious Bible scholars agree that it is enormously difficult to ascertain just what Jesus had to say on this subject. For he said something, something offensive, which his own pious disciples were unable to hear without choking, and which they did not transmit to us in its fullness. This is indeed a startling story. Let me illustrate it. An adulterous woman was caught in the act, and the self-righteous Pharisees brought her to Jesus to be stoned. The custom was that men were permitted everything but that a woman, if caught, was supposed to be stoned. You know what Jesus answered: "Let him who is without sin among you be the first to throw a stone at her" (R.S.V.). And the self-righteous Pharisees slunk away slowly, shamefacedly.

Now Bible scholars tell us that what Jesus thought about sex is contained in this story. But to ferret out the full truth about this story is in itself a disturbingly difficult enterprise. For it nearly got lost at the hands of the disciples; it is rather a wonder that it survived at all. As a matter of fact it does survive only in later manuscripts. We feel that the understanding, the magnanimity, with which Jesus viewed this woman deeply offended the disciples.

According to the biblical scholars, the chief service Jesus rendered in this painful matter was to set women free from the tyranny of men. If anyone has cause to be grateful to Jesus, it is women, because he rejected the tyranny which men held over them, a tyranny in which everything was permitted to men, whereas women were, for the same acts, supposed to be stoned. Jesus did not create a new code of laws at this point, but rather took women out of this inhuman position and gave them human dignity. It is not a coincidence that women looked upon Jesus with such reverence and adoration. Nor is it a coincidence that, in response to the words of Jesus, Mary Magdalene found it easy to forsake her dissolute life. They were ready to obey a man who would treat them as human beings and, for his sake, they were willing to begin a new life. But what Jesus taught in the matter of sexuality is very difficult to unravel. I will limit myself to the final result, the merest summary. What did Jesus say about sex and adultery?

He said, " 'But seek first his [God's] kingdom and his righteousness' [R.S.V.], and then all your problems, including problems of sex, will be solved." In modern language—the sexual instinct is a potent energy. By himself, man is powerless against it. No man is strong enough singlehandedly to win the victory over his sexual instinct. "But seek first his kingdom." This means that we must first enter a greater field of force. If we live in God's kingdom, our love life will fall into place in a pure and human way. To put it even more simply: If someone is possessed by the cause of God's kingdom, then love will not be a demonic force for him. It will rather be a beautiful passion, a holy obligation that will occupy his energies in the proper direction and toward glorious fruition. He who has no cause beyond himself makes sex his cause. Alas, I see even in this congregation men and women who have no other cause except to give free rein to sex, to their love life, or to spoil the love life of others. If they are incapable of happiness, at least they ought not to ruin the happiness of others. And all that in the name of God. There is nothing more repulsive than this.

Thus the solution is not for me to do anything. The solution rather is to fit into God's order, into God's kingdom, and *there* everything falls into place.

Without going into detail, let me just raise one more question: How do we interpret the commandment, "You shall not commit adultery," in the spirit of Jesus? If we look at this Old Testament commandment from Jesus' point of view, what is in it?

One—the original meaning and application are unchanged: Do not break into and ruin the love life of another.

Two—do not worship sex. Do not think that sex is the summit, the very best, for which it is worthwhile to sacrifice everything. There is more to life than sex.

Three—do not be afraid of sex. Do not fear it, do not let your sexual energy become demonic. Do not choke it off, or try violently to suppress it, because it is liable to explode your life.

Four—according to Jesus Christ, sexual energy is not designed merely to assure that there will be enough people on earth, but rather that man may become more human. Sex can be a divine help in the process of becoming human. To put it differently, sex exists not that there may be life on earth but that there may be joy in this earthly life. The Apostle Paul says that marriage testifies to Jesus Christ. And if that is true, which indeed it is, then it is also true that love testifies of salvation. Where love exists in truth, within God's order, there we have a mirror of salvation.

One more word—and I'm choosing my words carefully. Wherever sexual energy is being used in a joyful, releasing, redemptive way, there it is being used well. Wherever sexual energy is being used in an animalistic way for mutual violence and torture, there is adultery—even if there is a marriage certificate on hand. This is my final conclusion. And may God help us to understand his thought!

# VIII

## DO NOT TAKE—
## GIVE AWAY—
## WHAT IS NOT YOURS!

Exodus 20:15

"You shall not steal" (R.S.V.).

We have been talking about murderers and about adulterers. Some of you, I'm sure, are hoping that now it is the thieves' turn to get their comeuppance! Perhaps some of you are feeling a kind of national pain: "Woe to us, what has happened to our Hungarian people, since every one of us has become something of a thief." This is something we have to talk about!

Those of you who are thinking in this way are sitting in the grandstand and congratulating yourselves in your hearts: "My hands are clean; thank God, this does not concern me; I do hope that the pastor will really give it to the thieves."

Well, my sermon will be flunking badly if anyone goes home with the impression that thieves have at last got their comeuppance! It will be a damnably bad sermon if anyone feels left out of the circle of those whom God addresses with this commandment. I shall not hide my intention. I would like you to entertain some new thought as to what thievery or stealing is. Furthermore, I would like you to engage in self-examination as a result of these new thoughts. And finally, I would like you to begin a new kind of conduct as a result of this self-examination.

When discussing the commandment against adultery, we said that it is possible to walk with head held high in its presence as long as we do not take seriously the New Testament interpretation, "But I say to you that every one who looks at a woman lustfully has already committed adultery with her in his heart" (r.s.v.). If the New Testament thus deepens the question, if it places the smallest movement of the soul under God's judgment with respect to adultery, then it would surely do the same thing with respect to stealing. So if we accept the fact that the business of adultery cannot be settled on the basis of external conduct, it will be necessary for us to apply the same norm to this commandment. In the light of the entire Word of God, there is more at stake here than the little rhyme we used to write upon our rulers in school, "God's eyes see everything, DO NOT STEAL THIS RULER." More is at stake here than the question of whether or not I've actually touched and taken someone else's possession.

Let me offer a few illustrations. Someone has a great deal of time on his hands. So he imposes his presence upon another and thus steals the time of a man who has important work to do. In the eyes of God that is surely a theft of time, indeed the theft of a valuable man's time.

People enjoying gossiping, saying whatever comes to their minds without examining the facts of the case. Is this not stealing another person's *honor*? In God's judgment, honor is at least as important as a ruler. And just because gossiping is fun, is it any less of a theft?

Once I was in the company of a number of physicians where a young doctor boasted that he had discovered an effective drug. He said, however, that he was not going to share his secret with "this state," because here inventions are not adequately compensated and he was not going to be robbed. A debatable position. In any case, if this doctor knows something and does not make it available to the sick, he is in effect robbing thousands of people of the possibility of healing. And is this not stealing?

I think it is becoming apparent how wide the scope of this problem is. Let us go on, therefore, and open our hearts to a deeper understanding of the eighth commandment. Let us first try to un-

derstand the essence of stealing. To put it simply, *"I want more.
I have something, but it is little, and if the other will not willingly
share with me, I will take it away."* At the bottom of theft is a
hunger for life: "I want to lead a more complete life. To this end,
I need more of one thing or another, and, if I cannot secure it in
any other way, I will steal it." Or, "I want to live a richer life. For
that, I need what is yours, and I will take it, whether it be your
honor or your time or any other valuable possession." That is the
essence of stealing.

What is God's reaction to this? Many believers would answer,
in God's name, that God would command us to be content with
what we have—to be modest, undemanding, resigned; if, therefore,
you feel that there is something more you want in your life, call
this feeling sin, uproot it from your heart, and then you will not
steal.

This sounds good, and I'm not saying that it does not contain
some truth. However, I do not believe that this is essentially God's
thought. I would express God's thought in this way: "Man, you are
right in your desire for a richer life. I myself would have you live
an abundant life. You are right if you want more. But you are not
supposed to take this 'more' from others. You are supposed to
*create it yourself."* God's design for the enrichment of life is for
us to secure such enrichment through work, not through theft. And
this is different from what believers usually say. God's final thought
on the matter is not resignation, poverty, nothing. He wants us to
aspire to a higher, richer life. But he would have us understand that
the way to attain this richer life is not to rob others of their possessions but to secure it for ourselves by honest work.

But this good desire for a richer life has been distorted, so that
we think we can satisfy it by taking a shortcut, by stealing what
we need from others. We have been discussing the Ten Commandments throughout in terms of their contribution to the process of
becoming human. Now once more we find ourselves in this dimension. God's message to us is that man becomes human by enriching
his life through work. And that man enters a blind alley, loses his
way when he tries to enrich himself through stealing.

It is distressing how man stumbles amidst a variety of wrong
theories. I would like to comment on two such theories, from the

perspective of history. One is as bad as the other. The first flourished centuries ago in so-called Christian Europe. It was succeeded by another that does not lead to life either. The medieval Christian theory may be summed up by the phrase "the ideal of poverty." It was replaced by what we will call "the ideal of wealth." Wealth is as much an ideal today as poverty was in the Middle Ages. Our children adopt it without any particular training for it; they absorb it through the air. During the Middle Ages, the ideal of poverty was absorbed in the same way, by being linked to the concept of salvation. Its essence was that he who would obey God by voluntarily embracing poverty would be rewarded with salvation.

We need not deny that this outlook was harmful to mankind. When poverty, disorder, and dirt are the ideal, no hygiene, no medical science, no life, no abundance, will grow.

Then the ideal of wealth succeeded the ideal of poverty: The rich man is the man who counts. If you get rich, we will forget how you did it. Success legitimates the method. The ideal of wealth spawned inhumanity by logical necessity. For in practice, the ideal of wealth results in ruthlessness. It releases all the instincts of beasts of prey. It doesn't matter if I trample upon someone, if I rob him blind; the main thing is that I attain my goal—wealth. It is worthwhile to ponder how much of the energy of the nearly three billion people in today's world is devoted to the production of goods and how much of this energy is devoted to thieving, in which we may include the armaments race, industrial espionage, nuclear warfare, and all manner of technical preparation to enable us to rob one another. How much energy are we devoting to production and how much to arming ourselves in order to take away from others what is theirs? An appallingly large percentage of our energy is expended upon the robber instinct. A complex problem!

But let no one piously misinterpret the events of the history. We have to admit that not everything falls into the category of robbery. Sociologists and philosophers alike have come to realize that the rapid development of technology and the complication of the process of production may demand that which hitherto belonged to the individual to be brought under communal management. This cannot be construed as theft, even by the most serious Christian examination. Let me offer a simple example. Our Saint

Margaret's Island was for centuries someone's private property, obviously the property of an aristocrat, since they owned most of the land. They lived on the island, walked its length and breadth, and enjoyed themselves. Others were not permitted to set foot on it. This situation could be tolerated as long as few people lived in Budapest and nearly all of them had small garden plots. But with the city a major metropolis, and people crowded into apartment houses, it becomes inconceivable that—in 1966—a single family should possess the island of Saint Margaret! Would it not be robbery if all this beauty, all this fresh air, were withheld from our children? Frequently it is the satisfaction of a social need that brings on the communal management of something which used to be private property in a way that actually amounted to robbery over the generations. I'm saying this in order to keep us from making hasty judgments. Let us rather understand God's thought that we should have a rich life and that we should help one another to achieve such a life. It is God's thought that we should not enrich ourselves by robbing another, but by working and producing more and thus leading a more fully human life.

Martin Luther offers an excellent definition of the essence of stealing: "Whenever I secure some advantage at the expense of another, that is theft." It is conceivable that one could enjoy so much of society's goods that this would in effect harm others. And this can happen in any number of contexts—in the factory, in the family, or even in the life of a congregation—when one man achieves an advantage quickly and cheaply and in so doing deprives others. This is the essence of stealing.

Thus, to steal is not just to touch and actually take away what belongs to another. It is also not to give to another what is rightfully his, even though it is at present "deposited" with me. This is where the teaching of Scripture appears with graphic clarity. For the Bible speaks of *stewardship*. God has entrusted something to us. God has made us accountable for things, he has given them to us so that we in turn may pass them on. Whoever understands something of the secret of stewardship will readily accept the fact that stealing is not just touching and taking away what belongs to someone else, but also *not giving* to him what is really his rightful possession. God gave me more than I really need. If I don't circulate it, if I don't make it go around, if I don't use it for the enrichment of my life, in God's judgment I am a thief. He "who knows the good he ought to do and does not do it is a sinner" (N.E.B.), says the Apostle James. Whoever has something with which he might do good and does not do it becomes a thief.

Now let us expand this insight to global dimensions and then let us apply it more strictly to ourselves. It is my conviction that nations that surround their wealth with atom bombs are robber nations. And if the Hungarian people should choose so to protect themselves, the Hungarian nation would become a robber nation. Whoever protects his own rich life against the poor is a thief. God has entrusted to him a surplus which does not belong to him. He is supposed to pass it on, and God does not let the thieving of robber nations go unpunished.

And what makes sense in its global dimension also applies on the individual level. Any believer to whom God has granted religious experience, comfort, healing, who has received a great deal from God but is a coward and does not dare bear witness to these things before his fellowmen, is a thief. For God has given him something to pass on, but he is afraid, and does not. Thus his jealous guarding of his own life robs others of the possibility of comfort or healing. A cowardly believer who never talks about God is as much of a thief as are rich people. If he enjoys his own salvation and at the same time beholds people living in perdition all about him just because he dares not tell them that there is healing, there is hope—he is a thief!

Let me bring the message of the eighth commandment a little closer still. And I hope that when I am through you may all bow your heads and say, "God have mercy on us, thy thieving people, because we have been refusing thy gifts and living selfishly to ourselves." I'd like to tell you some painful observations about believers in relation to this matter of theft. There are three grades of theft of which believers are capable.

The first grade is the situation in which a believer robs God of himself. For we are God's property. In 1 Corinthians, chapter 6, we find these two verses: "Do you not know that your body is a temple of the Holy Spirit within you, which you have from God? You are not your own; you were bought with a price. So glorify

God in your body" (R.S.V.). "You are not your own; you were bought with a price." God bought you and you have become his possession. When we had gone astray and become slaves of sin, God redeemed us, bought us back, made us his own. The first level at which a believer commits robbery is when "he steals himself back" from God—as if he were his own, as if he were master of his money, his time, his faith, his knowledge.

We could talk at great length about our cleverness in rationalizing. Our powers of rationalization are truly amazing. The human intellect is indeed such a fine, well-wrought tool that we can explain everything. We can even explain how we manage our lives as if God had nothing to do with it. We abound in clever thoughts, the essence of which are rationalization of our disorder and disobedience. But you are here so that the voice of God's truth may sound forth over the din of human reasonings. And the truth is that God bought us—with the blood of Jesus. He brought us out of Egypt, then entered into covenant with us: "I, the Lord, am your God. I brought you out of mortal peril, out of nervous breakdown, out of material bankruptcy. And now I am saying to you, 'Do not steal!' I bought you for my own; do not steal yourself back from me!"

The second grade of theft to which believers are particularly prone is the sin of Achan, about which we have heard in our Scripture reading. Whoever withholds himself from God is obviously stealing for himself something which had been devoted to God. The first kind of theft is when we take back from God our whole life; the second is when we use for our own ends whatever God may have deposited with us for the sake, the benefit, of another, and which we do not really need for ourselves. This is the second grade of theft—to withhold things that have been designated for God. And because of this a curse rests on our lives. God says, "Don't complain to me. You're hiding in your tents and coffers what belongs to me. So there is a curse on you, and you will lose all your battles." We dare not use for our own advantage and enjoyment things which have been devoted to God.

And if a believer commits theft on these two grades, he is likely to go on to the third where his heart becomes hard. He is not interested. If the streetcar conductor doesn't say anything, he does not pay. And so the little thefts multiply—to the detriment of the state, of society. But it no longer matters, for the heart is hard. If we have stolen from God our whole life as well as many things which he has designed for others, then we will not be much concerned with the damage we are doing to them.

And if after hearing all these things, anyone can leave this place with his head held high, saying, "I thank God that I'm not like that, that my hands are clean, that I'm not a thief," it will be very sad indeed because it will show that he does not understand the first thing about God's truth. He does not understand that Jesus gave his life for him and thus redeemed him for God. He does not understand the Scriptures at all. May God have mercy on us and make sure that the message reaches our hearts.

Let us understand that there is a difference between the godly life and the life which pleases the devil. The life which pleases the devil is the life in which I want to be great and rich, in which I want to exploit others for my benefit. This is the devil's own motto. But the motto of the godly life can be found in the second chapter of the Letter to the Philippians. "Have this mind among yourselves, which you have in Christ Jesus, who, though he was in the form of God, did not count equality with God a thing to be grasped, but emptied himself . . ." (R.S.V.). Here runs a clear dividing line between the two ways of life. The devil's is characterized by exploitation. This is the spirit which pervades the world today. This is the spirit which is carrying the world toward appalling catastrophe. Production is a slow, labored process—to take away from another what he has produced yields quicker results. This frightful atmosphere pervades the whole world.

But God's way of life is summed up in Jesus Christ who, "though he was in the form of God, did not count equality with God a thing to be grasped, but emptied himself . . ."

May God bless us so that we may with penitence perceive the extent to which our souls are infected with the devil's way, the way of exploitation. And may God help us depart from this way by the spirit of Jesus Christ, who was rich but did not regard his wealth a thing to be grasped.

# IX

## YOU SHALL NOT BEAR FALSE WITNESS!

### Exodus 20:16

"You shall not bear false witness against your neighbor" (r.s.v.).

The ninth commandment speaks on three levels. According to its original and narrow meaning, it applies to giving testimony before a court of law: You shall not *bear false witness* against your neighbor before a judge.

On the second level, the commandment is usually expanded to mean: Do not *slander* your neighbor, whether you are standing before a judge or talking in the street. Watch your tongue! "How great a forest is set ablaze by a small fire!" (r.s.v.), says the Apostle James of the power of the tongue. Likewise, the Old Testament tells us that there is snake venom under the tongue. And it can indeed cause a great deal of misery and harm. Do not slander your neighbor! This is the second level.

And on the third level, the meaning of the commandment may be expanded even further: *Beware of lying!*

I shall concentrate upon the middle level, "Do not slander your neighbor!" This includes the narrower meaning that if by any chance you are summoned to testify in court, you should stick to the truth. But God's commandment applies to all of our life; therefore, we should consider it in the broader sphere. Not just in a court of law but in all our human relationships we should be careful to tell the whole and precise truth. Do not slander your neighbor! Do not trample upon your neighbor's honor!

It is hardly necessary to waste many words to prove how people love to gossip, to accuse each other, to slander each other. Remember your own circle of friends, your own conduct. If the conversation turns to someone's virtue, the subject is dull. But should it turn to his vices, things liven up at once. And we love to talk without checking on the facts. We love to pass on stories. It is exciting to be able to say something evil about another! There are people who are extremely sensitive about what is being said about them. They become indignant, angry; they lash out against anyone who has said anything unflattering about them. But these same people quite freely say bad things about others. We tend to be sensitive about our own honor but very indifferent to the honor of others. This is a well-known fact. It can be observed in any company, in any office, indeed in any congregation. We much prefer to gossip, to slander each other, than to bear good witness about each other.

What lies at the bottom of this universal human phenomenon? Whence this attitude? I've given the subject a great deal of thought and have succeeded at last in compressing my diagnosis into a single expression, "the prestige obsession." Slanderous conversation is born of an obsessive concern with prestige. What is prestige? We may call it self-worship, the cult of the self, an illusion of grandeur: "I am the center of the universe." Everyone is the victim of this misery to a greater or lesser extent. Everyone would like to stand out, be heard, rule over the rest. This is the desire, the instinct, which I chose to call "the prestige obsession," because it is a profoundly unhealthy phenomenon. I admit that it was God who gave man the desire to rise, to be great. That is not bad in itself —I believe that God created man for growth and greatness. But when concern with prestige becomes obsessive, there is trouble.

It happens this way: "I want to be great, but there is someone else around who does not let me because he seems to be greater than I am. He is competition. He is my rival. What can I do?" A healthy solution would be to outstrip him by honest work. This would be a good approach: "He is great, I too want to be great, therefore I will work harder and outshine him with greater accomplishment." This would, in addition, advance the progress of human society. But ordinarily we seek a cheaper solution: "If I cannot be as great as you are, I will throw mud at you in order to make myself greater! People will see that you are covered with mud!" Such a dastardly thing is slander.

Let us make this quite clear. The desire to advance one's self is all right. So let us create things, let us accomplish things. But sin begins when we refuse to shoulder the burden and fatigue of hard work and prefer the cheaper solution of trampling upon another's honor. This is the shame of slander—and it has a thousand varieties, some of them quite subtle and hard to discover. Indeed, Christians really have to work to discern the presence of this evil in their own heart.

To give an example: A man notices that his wife is attracted by another man. So that man becomes "a drip," "an idiot." Of course women do not take the back seat to anyone in this respect. A woman notices that another woman appeals to her husband. Instantly the other woman is "a stupid goose," "a scheming cat," or some other animal. The battle is on! We are throwing mud at the other so that we may be great.

This goes on collectively as well as individually. There is such a thing as a group spirit. Esprit de corps. We cannot stand the thought that our team may be less illustrious than the other. Unfortunately this happens in churches too. I got word that someone began to come to this church and was asked, "Are you going to go to church where a Communist minister is preaching?" All that counts is that our team be undefeated; truth does not count, Christ does not count: such can be the obsession with collective prestige.

It is my belief that obsessive concern with prestige causes a considerable amount of the suffering in the world. We cannot tolerate someone's outstripping us. This was the cause—at least the immediate cause—for the outbreak of World War I. We could not endure being insulted! We had to mobilize at once. There were other reasons too, I know.

I believe that it was because of the prestige obsession that Hitler was unable to conclude World War II when he had long since lost it. It was unthinkable that an empire whose ruler Hitler had been should suffer a loss of prestige.

And I'm very much afraid that prestige would play a large role in the outbreak of a third World War. The capitalists cannot tolerate the thought that a Communist may be the first man to set foot on the moon. The Communists cannot tolerate the opposite, and the great prestige struggle goes on. I'm convinced that in the case of the war in Vietnam, prestige plays a much larger part than does the happiness of that unfortunate people. It is for prestige considerations that America refuses to get out. And it is an insoluble problem because at the bottom of the phenomenon of prestige there is the obsession, "I am great, I am first, I will not allow my glory to be obscured."

This is what the ninth commandment is all about: Learn to retreat, even though it may be with a loss of prestige. It would be possible to bring about world peace at once if the great powers were willing to run this risk. Would not world peace be worth it? But who is able to do it? Here we are at the very essence of the commandment. A part of the Christian's struggle with his faith is directed precisely against the obsession of prestige, whether it occurs in a jealous woman or in the thinking of a great world power. There are Christians in the United States who think, "We may suffer a loss of prestige, but we will not become victims of the prestige obsession!" Are there people in this church who dare match this thought? Are there courageous people here who are willing to raise a voice against an ecclesiastical prestige obsession? We talk about church renewal, about a triumphal march, because the prestige of the church demands that we present ourselves to the world as victors. But he who would obey the ninth commandment will let the truth prevail. Thus we should stop telling lies, slandering each other, boasting, for the sake of prestige. If we persist in them, we will perish. Let the truth be heard. Are there people, here in this congregation, who out of faith are willing to wage war upon the prestige obsession? It is not easy. Whoever would participate in this struggle must first of all engage in a terrifying struggle with himself. And it is to this inward struggle with the demon of prestige that I would like to direct your attention now.

For it is true that we lie not only to one another, but to ourselves. Anyone who has not arrived at the point where he is honest with himself has no right to raise a voice against his fellowmen. Only he who has learned to be truthful with himself is able—quietly, resolutely—to testify to the world at large.

We may liken our inner world to a great parliament where debates and discussions are going on. Your inner life will be wholesome to the extent that it really is like a session of parliament, with an opposition. Your inner life will be healthy to the extent that it is filled with tension. However, it is difficult to live with tension, to debate with one's self, to judge one's self. So—and this has been thoroughly examined and beautifully elaborated by the psychologists—we develop ways in which to silence this parliamentary debate. We develop ways to adjust ourselves to others but to do so in good conscience.

Someone has described the situation by this clever parable. A stranger arrives in town. He has a watch which is wholly accurate. Upon his arrival, he looks at the clocks in the church steeples and finds that they are a half-hour fast. The people in town have set their watches by these clocks. The whole town is living in a faulty time system. So the stranger tries to tell them, "People, my watch is accurate. This is the truth." But they make fun of him, they hit him over the head, they mistreat him. In the end, he begins to wonder, "Maybe my watch is not accurate after all. Maybe they are right." And he resets his watch to conform with the watches of the townspeople.

Do you understand the story? The crowd is not right. The crowd is hardly ever right. Prophetic spirits, chosen individuals, sincere seekers of the truth, are right. Jesus Christ was right over against the multitude. But there is power in the crowd, and Jesus had to either accept the cross or adapt himself to them. The first thing we have to fight out is whether we will adjust our watches to the clock in the steeple if we are certain that our watches are accurate. But this demands some very sensitive conduct. I dare not be aggressive. I cannot change the whole world. But I can refuse to reset my watch to conform to the clock in the steeple if the clock is wrong. Whoever meekly submits to the taste, the desire, the passion, of the crowd deceives himself. And whoever is not able to fight it out, to stand fast by his own conviction even if standing fast means serious setbacks, is not likely to render great service to the kingdom of God or to the human community.

To seek truth within myself does not mean that I am right under all circumstances, but that God is right who calls me a sinner, who forever reveals me to myself. I am supposed to carry about God's truth rather than any fanaticism of my own. This is the heart of the ninth commandment, which speaks to what goes on inside me: "Do not lie to yourself! Do not pretend to be a morally irreproachable person when you know that there are impure desires in your heart. At least be honest with yourself."

"God is right: I am a wretched man"—this is the kind of truthfulness we must practice. Then we may be able to participate successfully in the struggle against the prestige obsession.

Now let us look at the matter from the standpoint of Jesus Christ. The Old Testament bears its witness, but we cannot stop there. We must examine this witness in the light of Jesus Christ. What does he have to say about the ninth commandment? In the Gospel of Matthew, chapter 26, we read about the attempt to incriminate Jesus.

> Now the chief priests and the whole council sought false testimony against Jesus that they might put him to death, but they found none, though many false witnesses came forward. At last two came forward and said, "This fellow said, 'I am able to destroy the temple of God, and to build it in three days' " (r.s.v.).

Yes, Jesus experienced what it felt like to be the target of false witness. Eventually it was this false witness which caused him to be condemned to death. This is New Testament truth, and it is from this standpoint that the Old Testament Word has to be approached.

If we review Christ's story we realize that it was sin against the ninth commandment, "You shall not bear false witness against your neighbor," which caused him to be condemned to death. And there are two conclusions we can draw from this. First, always think of slander, of false witness, as if you were doing it to Jesus Christ, as if the whip of your words were exploding on his back. If you strike me, that is not dangerous, but Jesus identifies himself with me when you bear false witness against me because he lived through it, he who wanted to help the whole world, who wanted to build a wondrous new temple for God, he was accused of wanting to destroy the Temple! I love the church, but there are some who say that I'm destroying the church. Jesus has a great deal of understanding for, and solidarity with, those against whom false witness is being borne.

The other conclusion is this. As Christians we will not trample upon the honor of another, and if our honor is being trampled upon we will not make a big production of it. Rather we will say, "We are in good company. This is how people dealt with the prophets."

Christians will be rightly repelled by loose accusations. Let us always ask when someone is speaking in this vein in our presence, "Is this based upon personal knowledge? Have you made sure? Or is it merely hearsay? If you have hard facts, come on, let us clarify things! But if it is only hearsay, stop talking!" The outpouring of falsehood must be stopped.

One of the great consolations of my life has been a Chinese proverb, now many thousands of years old, "People only throw stones at a tree if it is bearing sweet fruit." That is quite clear. No one will bother throwing stones at a tree that is not bearing fruit. So let us not act tragic if we're being slandered. It is not that dangerous. Jesus Christ was slandered, and so were the prophets and the apostles. Let us take note of the fact and return to the order of the day.

On the one hand, we hold as sacred the life, honor, privacy, of our neighbor: we will not trample upon him. On the other hand, if we are being trampled upon, we will not take it too tragically. For we stand before the judgment seat not of men but of God.

In Psalm 109 there is a wonderful verse with which I close. If anyone has ever suffered from being the butt of slander, I recommend verse 28 of this Psalm for his comfort: "O LORD . . . Let them curse, but do thou bless!" Christians may not participate in the prestige obsession.

I am a minister and I will not yield my honor to anyone! Or will I? Well, as a minister I am a ready target for any loose mouth that happens to be gaping at me. I know that I must hold as sacred the honor of my fellowmen, and that as a Christian I cannot find my greatest joys in my own honor. Thus, if I am being slandered, I must say, "Just think how much I could add to what you are saying about me!" For the greatest value for any Christian is grace. That is to say, God in his grace accepted me, a sinful man; and God is giving his blessing to me, a sinful man. It is difficult to understand this juxtaposition. On the one hand, the honor of my neighbor is sacred to me, I dare not touch it; on the other hand, in my own life the only thing that matters is the grace of God. "O Lord . . . Let them curse, but do thou bless!" If only I do not lose thy grace! If we resolve to live in this way, we will be obeying the ninth commandment in the spirit of our Lord Jesus Christ!

# X

## YOU SHALL NOT CONNIVE AGAINST YOUR NEIGHBOR!

1 Kings 21:1–16

Exodus 20:17

"You shall not covet your neighbor's house; you shall not covet your neighbor's wife, or his manservant, or his maidservant, or his ox, or his ass, or anything that is your neighbor's" (r.s.v.).

The traditional interpretation of the tenth commandment centers upon the concept of *coveting*. Preachers usually expound the theme that in the eyes of God not only our deeds count but also the thoughts and desires that are in our hearts. In other words, the sinful motions of hand or foot, obvious aggression, patent wrongdoing are not the only sins. It is possible to sin even while restraining our hands and feet from sin, as long as in our hearts there are sinful dreams, desires, yens. Thus the usual interpretation of the tenth commandment is based upon the words "You shall not covet." Its primary concern is with a process that takes place within the soul.

There is certainly a great deal of truth in this approach. It is true that God measures not with an external but with an internal measure. Many texts could be cited to support this truth. For example, in the first book of Samuel, chapter 16, verse 7, we read, ". . . for the LORD sees not as man sees; man looks on the outward appearance, but the LORD looks on the heart" (r.s.v.).

In the Letter to the Hebrews, chapter 4, verses 12-13, we read, "For the word of God is living and active, sharper than any two-edged sword, piercing to the division of soul and spirit, of joints

104

and marrow, and discerning the thoughts and intentions of the heart. And before him no creature is hidden, but all are open and laid bare to the eyes of him with whom we have to do" (R.S.V.).

Or, again, the Apostle James speaks in chapter 1, verses 13-15, of the origin of sin in this way, "Let no one say when he is tempted, 'I am tempted by God'; for God cannot be tempted with evil and he himself tempts no one; but each person is tempted when he is lured and enticed by his own desire. Then desire when it has conceived gives birth to sin; and sin when it is full-grown brings forth death" (R.S.V.).

Or let us recall the ancient story of the first fall into sin, the forbidden tree and its desirable fruit. The Scriptures give a graphic description of how the woman looked upon the fruit of the forbidden tree and, to put it into modern idiom, wanted it so badly that her mouth began to water. And the desire became so intense that eventually it moved her body to take a piece of fruit from the tree and eat it.

Ministers then who preach that desire is dangerous, that God puts his claim upon us at the point of desire rather than only at our accomplished deeds, are indeed right. But the question is, "Is this what the tenth commandment is saying, or is it saying something slightly different?"

On the basis of what Old Testament scholars have discovered for us, we must acknowledge that this is not precisely the message of the tenth commandment. Let me tell you briefly what the scholars consider to be the original meaning and content of this commandment. They tell us that we should not focus our interpretation entirely upon one word. There are two words in the commandment which together express the original meaning. One of the words is indeed "covet." The other is "neighbor." This word is extremely important, because it occurs three times. Thus the whole meaning of the commandment must be derived from an understanding of the words "covet" and "neighbor." The most exciting question has to do with the precise meaning of the Hebrew word for "covet." The original word is *chamad*. According to the scholars, *chamad* means to connive until one manages to take possession of whatever it is one wants. One exerts himself, one manipulates things, until one attains his goal. Thus we see that more than just "desire" is at stake here. When we say, "You shall not covet," we are talking about a craving that unfolds deep within the soul but, according to the scholars, the Hebrew word connotes a certain activity as well. "You shall not covet" is something quite different from "You shall not *connive* until you have reached your goal and taken possession of whatever it is you covet." So the scholars contend that the message of the commandment goes beyond "You shall not covet"; that it is directed at the activity that follows desire, that it warns us against conniving until our desire is satisfied. Let us remember the words of the Apostle James, "God . . . himself tempts no one; but each person is tempted when he is lured and enticed by his own desire." He goes on to say, "Then desire when it has conceived gives birth to sin." Thus the tenth commandment does not emphasize desire so much as it emphasizes the activity which desire conceives. So the full meaning of the word *chamad* is: If you covet something, do not begin to exert yourself, to try by fair means or foul, to acquire it.

Usually our conniving is directed at maintaining the appearance of lawfulness while trying to possess the object of our desire. We try to maintain the appearance of legality while taking possession of something that it would be simple robbery for us to take otherwise. I would like to point out again then that the meaning of the Hebrew word concerns primarily our machinations.

Of course the concept of neighbor is equally important here because the conniving is directed against him. One tries to set things up in such a way that one will be in a position to take away from one's neighbor what belongs to him. This is why we read the story of Naboth—it demonstrates what we are talking about in a classical manner, the connection between desire and conniving.

The king covets the little plot of vineyard which adjoins his garden. He wants it and he asks Naboth for it. But Naboth is a faithful, simple, honest Jew. He says, "God gave it to me; I cannot let you have it." King Ahab goes home, sulking and bitter. He wanted something and he was not able to get it. So he lies down with his head toward the wall, he refuses to eat. He's acting like a sulking child. He is very much upset by the matter. Then along comes his wife, Jezebel, the wicked pagan queen, and she says to him, "Why make so much of a little thing? The problem can be solved!" Jezebel begins to connive. She writes to the elders of the people, "Start a lawsuit against Naboth because he has cursed God and the king. Then have him stoned." Jezebel is conniving to take care of the matter with the appearance of legality. And, of course, false witnesses are found against Naboth, the suit runs its course, and he is taken outside of town and stoned to death. Then Jezebel triumphantly reports to the king, "Well, occupy the land!"

This story demonstrates in a quite awesome way what the tenth commandment is all about. It has more to say about Jezebel, in fact, than it does about King Ahab. Ahab coveted Naboth's vineyard but was not able to get it; so he began to sulk. That was not the real sin. The real sin began when Jezebel started to connive. The tenth commandment does not say, "Don't be like Ahab." It does say, "Don't be like Jezebel," who connived to get the vineyard and got it. Desires are born in our hearts, they cannot be presented. Thus the real sin is not the desire but rather the machinations which follow upon desire. And this is where the neighbor comes into the picture.

Naboth had been a loyal subject of the king, a good neighbor to him. Thus, in order to take his vineyards from him, it would be necessary to make him appear as a blasphemer, as the king's enemy. It would be necessary to obscure the concept "neighbor" so that Naboth would appear no longer as neighbor but as enemy. Should this attempt succeed, it would then be possible to have him stoned to death and take away all his possessions.

Thus we see now more clearly what the biblical scholars are telling us. The tenth commandment speaks to us on two levels. On the first level we are warned against conniving. On the second level we are urged to look out for our neighbor, lest our machinations cloud the concept of "neighbor." Remember how the question "Who is my neighbor?" was put to Jesus. People were indeed thinking, as Jesus reminded them, "You shall love your neighbor and hate your enemy" (R.S.V.). Therefore as soon as I can establish the belief that someone is not my neighbor but my enemy, I earn the right to do him harm. And we constantly manipulate this concept of neighbor. This is why the tenth commandment says, "You shall not connive against your neighbor."

Think of Jesus Christ. How Caiaphas had to connive before he was able to present him to the crowd as a blasphemer, a destroyer of the Temple. How he had to connive to present him to the Roman governor as a rebel against Caesar and opposed to paying Caesar tribute. How he had to connive to make Jesus out to be a villain. But in the end he was successful. He did not rest until Jesus was crucified. This was his sin, that he coveted Jesus' knowledge, power, popularity, and that he then connived until Jesus was nailed to a cross. "Who is my neighbor?" Do not do any tricks with the concept of neighbor!

There is a good contemporary word to describe the activity by which we manage in our hearts to put another in a disadvantageous position. It is *discrimination*. In its simplest form, the tenth commandment says, "You shall not discriminate." The essence of discrimination is to pass judgment upon another in an invidious way so that I will be able to push him aside, to put some stamp of reproach upon him so that I may take away what belongs to him: his house, his wealth, whatever I happen to covet. The tenth commandment is against discrimination. And it is an unbelievably timely commandment. For there are so many kinds of discrimination in the world that it is impossible even to begin to enumerate them. And the essence of all discrimination is the notion that someone is not fully reliable, therefore we have to take over his possessions; that he is an enemy, therefore he has to be put in jail; that he is not a human being, he is not a friend, he is not my neighbor, therefore he does not have the right to live. It is against this attitude that God says, "Do not connive against him, because he is your neighbor."

When the people asked Jesus, "Who is my neighbor?" this was a very concrete problem. For it was assumed that one had religious obligations toward the neighbor but none toward anyone else. Therefore it was necessary to determine who the neighbor was. The definition of neighbor was limited: only Jews were neighbors. Thus it was against the law to covet the house of a Jewish neighbor. Of course it was all right to take away someone else's. Or one might say, "Only he who keeps the Sabbath, the law of the Sabbath, is

my neighbor. Those who do not may be Jews, but they are not
neighbors." Discrimination was going on all the time, and the circle
within which human obligations prevailed was being drawn ever
more closely. For there were not supposed to be any orders from
God with respect to outsiders. It was against this background that
people approached Jesus with the question "Who is my neighbor?"
And in response to the question, Jesus told the story of the merciful
Samaritan, which threw into bold relief the truth that the very one
against whom you feel like discriminating is your neighbor. Even
the Samaritan, whom you consider racially inferior, is your neighbor, just as he in effect confesses, to the shame of the Jews, that
he regards them as his neighbors. It is the intention of Jesus that
we should give up discrimination, and regard as our neighbor whoever lives alongside us.

But Jesus goes even further: "But I say to you, 'Love your
enemy and pray for those who persecute you . . .' " (R.S.V.).

There is a popular saying, "Look out; today's friend may be
tomorrow's enemy." In other words, don't trust your friend too
much because tomorrow he may take advantage of whatever you
may have told him today. Jesus turns this popular wisdom around
and says, "Risk something; for by taking a risk, today's enemy may
become tomorrow's friend." When Jesus says, "Love your enemy,"
he is not preaching sentimentality. He does not mean that, as a
matter of self-protection, we should not strike out at another, since
he may be stronger; or that we should love him with just any kind
of love. Jesus says the exact opposite: "Fight so that hostility may
be overcome through love." Jesus says, "Love your enemy," which
means that we should take some loving initiative toward him in the
hope that, should it be effective, the enmity itself might cease.

There are three courses of action which must be considered in
order to raise our understanding of the tenth commandment from
an Old Testament plane to the full light of Christ. The first course
of action is conniving—how to get more and more out of my neighbor so that I may have more and more. For I am the one who
counts, and he exists in order to let me have things.

The other course of action is in effect inaction, that I do him
no harm, nor do I do him any good. He does not concern me. For
me, he is like the air—it is as if he did not exist. This is a rather

prevalent attitude among men today. We're tired of hostility and afraid of friendship. So we pretend that others are not there.

The third course of action represents God's part in the matter. "Love your neighbor." Do something for the other. People's actions are generally reactions—not in the political but in the psychological sense of the word. We respond to stroking with stroking, to vindictiveness with vindictiveness. As is the action, so is the reaction. In a way, this is what underlies the so-called truth that is summed up in the words "an eye for an eye, a tooth for a tooth"; but this is not the Christian attitude. God's thought is that we should initiate some action. Indeed, if someone has started a harmful action against you, it is God's thought that you should at once initiate a friendly, peace-making action. To be a Christian means that we may not react mechanically. We may not respond according to the findings of psychology, but *distinctively*. So we receive our strength from a peculiar source that enables us to react in unexpected ways.

People resemble the soldiers in World War I who dug themselves into trenches. The rifles were aimed at the trenches opposite, and if anyone dared to climb out or even to stick out his head, a volley followed. This is a static war, a trench war. And this is what is going on in the world. People dig themselves into some trench of hostility and then watch for any hostile move in the other trench. If one occurs, there is an exchange of fire, and then again retreat. But Jesus says, "Come out of your trenches! Expose yourself to a volley or two. Get out and extend a hand of peace!" This is risky business, but this is what it means to be Christian: to stop the trench warfare, to come out, to approach each other with goodwill, to stretch out a friendly right hand, to offer reconciliation.

The Old Testament then is negative, "Do not connive against your neighbor." Jesus puts it positively, "Regard even your enemy as your neighbor and win him over." Or to put it differently, the Old Testament said, "Do not discriminate against anyone." But the New Testament proclaims a gospel precisely to those who are being discriminated against. There is a message of joy in the gospel for the little ones, the rejected ones, the shortchanged ones, the sinful ones, the unworthy ones. To them it is announced that, unlike the high priests and the emperors, God does not discriminate against them; rather, he receives them with love, sick and sinful as they are.

It is interesting how the thought of the two Testaments harmonizes. The Old Testament says it dimly: "Do not do this wicked thing. Do not discriminate." Jesus says, "If you are being discriminated against, do not despair, because the love of God is addressed first of all to such." And if God accepts you who have been discriminated against, it is so that you may become his partner in the demolition of all dividing walls. But if this is so, then it is particularly awful to find among believers an attitude which says in effect, "We are being saved. You are being damned, you will burn in the fires of hell." This is a wicked thing, and believers must stop it. It is true that God accepts those who have been discriminated against, but he does not expect them to indulge in counter-discrimination! Rather, he sends them out to become brothers among brothers and take down all dividing walls of hate, so that men may at last become brothers. The tenth commandment says, "Do not discriminate," but Jesus adds, "If you are being discriminated against, God loves you. He comforts you, and he sends you back in the world so that you may be busy taking down all dividing walls."

Thus we have come to the end of the Ten Commandments. Let me conclude with a thought which may summarize what I have been trying to say. What are the Ten Commandments and how should we believers look upon them? I will again put it in the form of a parable.

The Ten Commandments are not a collection of medical prescriptions: "Do this, and you will be healed; and you will be all right." No, the Ten Commandments are rather a *compass* which shows the direction in which we must seek the solution. We misuse them if we treat them like prescriptions for salvation. We treat them rightly if we find in them spiritual guidelines, if we follow the spiritual direction that God reveals to us through them.

We may ask, "What is wrong morally with the world? Is it that people know what is right but are not willing to do it?" If that is the case then perhaps there is room for scolding: "You wicked people, you know the truth but you refuse to do it!" But, friends,

I confess that it is my conviction that this is not the moral predicament. The moral predicament of the modern world is that *we do not know what is right.* Our norms have become confused. According to my observation, contemporary man really does not know what is right or what is wrong. Therefore there is really no room for scolding. On what account can you scold the blind man if he bumps into a table? In most cases, modern man sins without ever having glimpsed the true, the good. Thus, in our modern predicament, the Ten Commandments have an enormous significance. Acting as a compass rather than a collection of prescriptions, they point us *in the direction of humanity.*

The significance of the Ten Commandments is that they point the way. By themselves, they do not secure salvation. But for this pointing of the way two things are necessary, and they are both gifts of the Holy Spirit. In order to be guided by the Ten Commandments in the proper direction, it is necessary to have the actual guidance of the Holy Spirit. It is the Holy Spirit who makes small change of the large bank notes that are the Ten Commandments. It is he who must direct us in concrete problems on the basis of the broad guidelines the commandments offer. If I fall silent before God, his Spirit can give me specific *light* as to what to do with respect to theft, or marriage, or neighbor love. There is no substitute for this concrete guidance by the Holy Spirit. Neither churchly casuistry nor sermons are a substitute for it. And this is one thing we need.

The other thing we need is the *power* of the Holy Spirit. For it does indeed happen that I glimpse the truth in all its brightness and am still impotent to carry it out. This is how a congregation gathered around the name of Jesus Christ must deal with the Ten Commandments: They must follow the light in the direction God's compass points. God's compass signals the direction, but within this direction we need the concrete commands and the power of his Holy Spirit in order to be enabled to move forward.

May God bless us so that we may not be content merely to reflect the light which we have received but to do the concrete deeds toward which it points us. Let us pray for the light of the Holy Spirit and above all for the power of the Spirit so that we may be enabled to walk in this path. Amen.